WHAT JERUSALEM MEANS TO US
Jewish Perspectives and Reflections

Edited by
Saliba Sarsar and Carole Monica C. Burnett

JPI

A Publication of
The Jerusalem Peace Institute

Holy Land Books
An imprint of
N B P Noble Book Publishing Incorporated
N. Bethesda, MD

Library of Congress Control Number: 2023933688
ISBN: 978-1-7320286-5-4
EBOOK: 978-1-7320286-6-1
First edition

Holy Land Books
An imprint of
Noble Book Publishing Incorporated
11200 Rockville Pike
Suite 405
N. Bethesda, MD 20852
www.noblebookpublishing.com

Published in the United States of America

CONTENTS

PREFACE
Rateb Y. Rabie

Jerusalem is widely regarded as the center of the world because it is sacred to Judaism, Christianity, and Islam and their followers. For centuries, the world's different traditions have shared, fought over, built, and rebuilt the Holy City.

We all belong to Jerusalem, and it belongs to us. Each of us relates to her in different ways—religiously, spiritually, culturally, historically, politically, socially, psychologically, and financially, or a combination thereof.

This book, *What Jerusalem Means to Us: Jewish Perspectives and Reflections*, illuminates Jewish connections to and views on Jerusalem. Its main goal is to educate, clarify, and celebrate what it is about this Holy City that Jews hold dear. The contributors to this book embody the spirit of sharing and believe, like most others, that Jerusalem is also home to Christians and Muslims.

What Jerusalem Means to Us: Jewish Perspectives and Reflections is published by the Jerusalem Peace Institute (JPI) (https://www.jerusalem-pi.org), which highlights Jerusalem as humanity's shared gift, governed by two peoples and cherished by three faiths, and its centrality for a just peace. See Appendix I. This book follows on the successful publication of *What Jerusalem Means to Us: Christian Perspectives and Reflections* (https://hcef.org/publications/what-jerusalem-means-to-us/) and of *What Jerusalem Means to Us: Muslim Perspectives and Reflections* (https://hcef.org/publications/what-jerusalem-means-to-us-muslim-perspectives-and-reflections/), which were published by the Holy Land Christian Ecumenical Foundation (HCEF) in 2018 and 2021, respectively.

The aforementioned three books will constitute the *Jerusalem Trilogy*, representing a true expression of our commitment to Jerusalem and its inhabitants. I urge people of good will—Jews, Christians, Muslims, and others—to advocate for maintaining the city as an inclusive center of faith; to preserve its religious Status Quo; and to sustain it as home to Jewish Israelis, Palestinian Christians and Muslims, and others.

Finally, I would like to express my deep gratitude to Dr. Saliba Sarsar and Dr. Carole Monica C. Burnett for their hard work on assembling and editing this important volume.

Rateb Y. Rabie
Co-Founder and Chairman of the Board of Directors
  Jerusalem Peace Institute
Founder and President/CEO
  Holy Land Christian Ecumenical Foundation

INTRODUCTION
Saliba Sarsar

Jerusalem is a distinctive city for Judaism, Christianity, and Islam and their adherents. It is equally special for millions of Jews and Arabs worldwide, for Israelis and Palestinians, who revere it and regard it as a precious inheritance from their ancestors, spiritual or physical or both.

For the Jewish connection to Jerusalem, the main subject of this volume, Jerusalem stands as the heart of Judaism and Jewish consciousness. It is mentioned more than 660 times in the Hebrew Bible and called by 70 names, among which are Shalem, meaning "whole" or "at peace"; City of God; City of Truth; Oasis of Justice; and Light of the World.

Jerusalem is the focus in prayer and ritual. Jews pray facing Jerusalem, the common Mother City, the Gate to Heaven. "Next Year in Jerusalem" (*L'Shana Haba'ah B'Yerushalayim*) is usually sung at the conclusion of the Passover Seder and of the *Ne'ila* service on Yom Kippur (Day of Atonement), the holiest day in Judaism. After meals, Jews recite a prayer that highlights Jerusalem: "Have mercy Lord, our God... on Jerusalem Your city, on Zion the resting place of Your glory..." and "Rebuild Jerusalem, the holy city, soon in our days. Blessed are you, God, who rebuilds Jerusalem in His mercy, Amen."

Psalm 122—attributable to King David, but possibly to a pilgrim who experienced Jerusalem—is a song of ascents, a song of praise and prayer. Verses 5-9 state:

Pray for the peace of Jerusalem:
    "May they prosper who love you;
Peace be within your walls,
    and security within your towers."
For the sake of my relatives and friends
    I will say, "Peace be within you."
For the sake of the house of the Lord our God,
    I will seek your good.

Jerusalem is also the geographic center of Jewish history. Jews associate key historical-religious events with Jerusalem and the region. These include Abraham's journey from Ur to Canaan in ca. 1900 BCE; David uniting the twelve tribes of Israel, and his son Solomon building the First Temple in Jerusalem in ca. 1000 BCE; Judah conquered by Babylon, the First Temple destroyed, and the inhabitants exiled to the conquering empire in 586 BCE; and the Romans destroying the Second Temple in 70 CE, leaving only a part of the Western Wall, and deporting part of the Jewish people from historic Palestine.

In exile, the Israelites lamented over the destruction of Jerusalem:

If I forget you, O Jerusalem,
    let my right-hand wither!
Let my tongue cling to the roof of my mouth,
    if I do not remember you,
if I do not set Jerusalem
    above my highest joy. (Psalm 137:5-6)

Additionally, Jerusalem has ideological and political significance to Jewish Israelis and to Jews worldwide. A symbol of self-determination and national independence, its possession and safety are paramount. This is anchored in the Zionist vision and program to establish for the Jewish people "a publicly and legally assured home in Palestine," especially in Zion or Jerusalem, as was decided at the First Zionist Congress, which met in Basel, Switzerland, in August 1897 and as was expressed in the Balfour Declaration in November 1917. The vision became a reality in May 1948, when the Zionist movement declared the creation of the Jewish state, Israel. It also accounts for Israel's policies and actions, mainly its constant efforts to Judaize Jerusalem and ensure Jewish dominant presence there.

What Jerusalem Means to Us: Jewish Perspectives and Reflections addresses the intimate and unique connections among Jews, Judaism, and Jerusalem along a variety of dimensions—religious, spiritual, historical, cultural, political, psychological, and social. These are manifested through the perspectives and reflections of sixteen Jewish leaders representing different backgrounds. The resultant essays present a rich array of personal and professional transformations, extraordinary love and hope for Jerusalem, as well as an honest appraisal of some of the challenges of daily living. What follows provides glimpses or insights from each author's contribution.

Yael S. Aronoff reflects on what Jerusalem means to her personally, as well as to Jews as a people. Following a quick rendition of the historical and religious bonds to the city, she shares her views on life in Jerusalem where "[m]y soul feels free in Jerusalem," where "I feel at home there." While Jerusalem is Aronoff's "favorite city in the world," given its great beauty, diversity, and celebrations, she is fully cognizant of the cleavages, tensions, and sadness resultant from differences between ultra-Orthodox Jews and secular and traditional Jews on one hand and between Palestinians and Jewish Israelis on the other, themes that are touched upon by other authors. A strong advocate for the two-state solution, Aronoff has hope for reaching accommodation over Jerusalem, one that "would continue to enable Jews to exercise their deepest connections to Jerusalem, while also exercising Jewish (and universal) values that would support self-determination for Palestinians as well as Jews."

Naamah Kelman writes of the religious connections of the Jewish faith and people to Jerusalem. It is in many blessings, prayers, and rituals that the Holy City takes form. As a liberal religious Jew who lives in today's Jerusalem, she is fully aware of the complexity and the divisiveness of its reality, which make conversations and coexistence hard. Yet, there is hope, as witnessed in the Israeli health system, where residents cooperate and are treated together, as well as in the peacebuilding field where institutions or organizations work for the creation of a shared society. Kelman asks of us to reach out to the other. "Until we can all see one another, until we can hear the multiple stories and attachments," she writes, "we will live in a beautiful but disputed, disjointed city." She further suggests, "If we succeed in reaching out to the other, perhaps, like the broken glass that ends each Jewish wedding, we can sweep the pieces together, and fire them once more in a new form, shimmering for all."

Jerusalem also figures large in the life of Peretz Rodman. Aside from being a city of dreams and dreamers, Jerusalem brings all Jews together regardless of their differing backgrounds and religious affiliations. The city is "not so much one bastion of Jewish culture [but] an archipelago of Jewish lifestyle choices... [and] a carnival of Jewish options." Making his life in Jerusalem for the past four decades, Rodman is constantly reminded of "his place in the long sweep of Jewish history." Nevertheless, he is aware of neighbors "who are 'other,' who see the world differently, who live according to another calendar." The city's diversity and division have not diminished his deep attraction and connection to it. Having grown up in Boston with the assumption that he would live his entire life in Massachusetts, he made Jerusalem his home instead, as "my consciousness of where home is for me shifted [in Jerusalem] to match what had been in my heart already."

John L. Rosove writes with candor of a divided city that is among "the most complex amalgams of faiths, cultures, peoples, and politics in the world." Aside from the perennial conflict between Israeli Jews and Palestinian Arabs, there is a fault line between ultra-Orthodox Haredi Jews and secular-non-Orthodox Jews. This basically relates to ultra-Orthodox Haredi men who try to impose their own will or version of Judaism on others at holy sites, for example, the Kotel or Western Wall, and become offended when seeing Jewish women carrying Torah scrolls and praying with men. Such a reaction runs counter to the principle of gender equality in Judaism and religious pluralism in Israel, as written in the Declaration of Independence. While he wonders if a unified Jerusalem is possible, he calls for sensitivity to others "who claim her as their own, because Jerusalem belongs to them too."

Laurence P. Malinger experienced the Holy City when he undertook his rabbinical studies at the Hebrew Union College-Jewish Institute of Religion's Jerusalem campus. At this time, he explored the Holy City, with its intertwined ancient and modern connections. Ideally, for him, the city would be "a place that enables many to live together in wholeness, or peace. This is what connects me strongly to this sacred city: the potential to be a place where everyone can get along, even with differing beliefs." Like John L. Rosove, a concern he raises as a Reform Jew emanates from the attitude of the ultra-Orthodox community that "rejects my Jewish expression as valid and meaningful." Regardless, he dreams of "a new era, [that] is not yet here." He concludes, poetically, "Like Jerusalem of Gold, its outline sits on the horizon just beyond our reach. And yet, in the darkness of the night its light still beckons. Distant as it is, it beckons us to draw near, as we ever so slowly approach to greet the dawn."

When Yehezkel Landau found his way to Jerusalem from America in the late 1970s, he chose to put his body where his Jewish prayers had already taken him. Like a magnet, the Holy City attracted him, and he reciprocated by contributing all he could to transforming discord into accord and exclusion into inclusion, particularly by promoting Jewish-Christian-Muslim engagement and Israeli-Palestinian peacebuilding for more than four decades. The primary challenge for Landau (and all of us) is how to enable Jerusalem to actualize "its vocation as the City of Peace." The solution rests with the different religious communities of Jews, Christians, and Muslims joining their hands and hearts in consecration while, simultaneously, the two national communities of Israelis and Palestinians would agree to share political sovereignty over the city. In a sense, peace materializes for one when it materializes for all.

Also making Jerusalem his home in the late 1970s is Ron Kronish. In time, he discovered both the ideal and the real Jerusalem and dedicated his life to bringing them closer together. After co-founding the Interreligious Coordinating Council in Israel, which he directed for 24 years, he was engaged intensively with Jews, Christians, and Muslims throughout the city, as well as with diverse groups of Palestinian Arabs and Israeli Jews to plan and implement dialogue and peace action projects. Pluralism, inclusiveness, holiness, justice, and peaceful coexistence, characteristics of the Heavenly Jerusalem, provided the vision for the Earthly Jerusalem.

For Jonathan Golden, some of the most formative and transformative moments of his life occurred in Jerusalem. In fact, he attributes much of who he is and the work he does to experiences he had and things he learned in the Holy City. His encounters there—the boy with the goat, the evening with young, hopeful Palestinians, and the week of terror attacks—moved him to do all that he could to advance peace in the region and to redirect his career in academia in the service of the common good. According to Golden, zero-sum thinking has led to unfortunate results. Jewish renewal in the land does not mean the dispossession of others. "Jewish return need not entail the erasure of others. If we all take a more magnanimous approach, we see that diverse claims to the city are not necessarily mutually exclusive. Presence without primacy."

Born in Jerusalem and raised in the neighborhood of Rehavia, Tamar Verete-Zahavi reflects on her early childhood there and tries to reconstruct the process of coming to understand that once in West Jerusalem there were Arab inhabitants. Their beautiful houses and fruit-filled orchards still beautify parts of the city. She poses many questions—"Who were the Arabs that escaped from their properties? Were they my enemies? Was it moral to live in their 'abandoned' houses? Would they come back?"—which ultimately became the building blocks of her political infrastructure as a young girl and as an adult. The childhood images she had of Jerusalem and the national identity she embodied disintegrated as new information entered her consciousness about the Nakba (the Palestinian Catastrophe) and the 1967 War, among other occurrences. In addition to considering the Palestinians as the genuine natives of the land, she "suddenly realized that life could change in one day … [and] that our stable daily life is reversible."

Elan Ezrachi ties his family's history to the evolution of Jerusalem, specifically its western part. From the arrival of his paternal grandfather from Odessa to Palestine under Turkish rule, to his father's birth in the Jerusalem neighborhood of Rehavia during the British Mandate, and to his own birth during the first decade of Israel's existence, we read of the expansion and transformation of West Jerusalem. The June 1967 War, during which Israel took over East Jerusalem (in addition to the West Bank, Gaza Strip, Sinai Peninsula, and Golan Heights), resulted in Israel asserting its control by huge construction projects and the settlement of Jews in the newly conquered areas. "New roads, archeological excavations, a new national holiday (*Yom Yerushalayim*), naming streets and sites in Hebrew—all were aimed at creating an irreversible reality." His preference is for Jerusalem to be "a liberal, Western-oriented place … not a site of controversy and dispute."

In his essay, Ilan Peleg provides a scholarly perspective on Jerusalem. After describing the moderate Zionist position on the centrality of Jerusalem, he analyzes the changes in the dominant Zionist perspective on Jerusalem brought about by the 1967 War, highlighting the emergence in Israel of a particularistic outlook associated with the Zionist Right and the subsequent marginalization of a more universalist outlook that has been present in traditional Zionist thought and action from their beginning. Further, after describing the "triumphalist" policies that were adopted by successive Israeli governments and City administrations toward Jerusalem, he presents an alternative policy that promotes the pursuit of justice in Jerusalem. While this policy is laudable, it could only be done by a creative process that is also cognizant of the difficulties in the real world.

Sharon Rosen, born into a Modern-Orthodox Jewish family in London, made *aliya* with her family following the 1967 war. Returning to her beloved Jerusalem after sojourns in apartheid South Africa and in conflict-ridden Ireland, she became aware of the Palestinian people who live on the land and value it equally. Her awakening focused on answering two questions: "What does it mean for two peoples to find the same land holy, to feel this umbilical attachment, and how can we find a way to live together without violent conflict?" Her answers make clear that "brandishing the message of exclusive ownership cannot be a solution to ending violence." For Rosen, "Jerusalem is a city of beauty, of pain, and of Messianic potential to be a beacon of light and peace to the billions who hold it dear." Capturing the light necessitates that we sustain hope and create paths to peace so that Jerusalem can achieve its promise and be the joy of the whole earth.

Menachem Klein lived most of his life in Jerusalem. Like most Israeli Jews, his perspective on the city and its Palestinian inhabitants changed over the decades. The First Intifada, the Oslo Accords, the reality on the ground, and interactions with Palestinians—all led him to move beyond the myth of "a united Jerusalem" and of Palestinians as "passive, an echo of the past, a friendly, charming stranger." His answer to the Jerusalem dilemma resides in Arab neighborhoods and the Haram al-Sharif being under Palestinian sovereignty and Jewish neighborhoods and the Western Wall being under Israeli sovereignty. Moreover, Jerusalem should have "open or very easy border crossings" as free movement of people and goods, along with cultural exchange and interpersonal encounter, creates and maintains thriving cities. Ultimately, what would engender peace is the acknowledgment that the "City of Justice" belongs to "all its residents equally. All must care about the place, and their everyday life perspective must be preferred over external interests and preserved."

Alice Rothchild writes of her evolving awareness from understanding Jerusalem's religious and historical significance to Jews and loving Israel uncritically to reconsidering many myths she heard at home and in Hebrew School. This change materialized as she began to examine "the price of the triumphal Jewish narrative of 'return' and 'unification' and the consequences of a perceived eternal Jewish victimhood that gave birth to the belief that historic Palestine was 'ours' at any cost." Jerusalem's exceptional appeal increased her inquiries:

"Why do Jewish Israeli claims take precedence over everyone else who has inhabited the city? Why do the needs and demands of Jews who have emigrated from Warsaw, Poland, or Brooklyn, New York, negate the claims of families who have actually lived in the city for centuries? What is the price of these policies for Jews as well as Palestinians?" Her answer expresses despair and hopelessness as she sees "the demise of decency and tolerance in an historic city that could have been shared amongst three Abrahamic faiths and might have been an example for the rest of the world."

Aleen Bayard shares her transformation that occurred during three trips to Jerusalem. Her first trip as a nine-year-old anchored her Jewish identity and enhanced her sense of heritage. Her second trip as an adult was influenced by the right-wing perspectives of the tour guide. It was during her third trip, a dual narrative tour organized by Medji tours, that she learned not only of Jewish events and tragedies, such as the destruction of the Temple and the Holocaust, but also of Palestinian events and tragedies, such as the Nakba, the Catastrophe, that befell the Palestinians in 1948 and caused their dispossession. Bayard came to appreciate the city as "a visceral paradox of hope and hopelessness, of sacred prayer and naked hostility, of unity and division." Amid unspeakable acts of revenge and violence, she met heroes and heroines engaging in peacebuilding and began to see the city through the eyes of both Israelis *and* Palestinians. She completes her essay by affirming that "Jerusalem is a holy place for all in the Holy Land."

For Martin J. Raffel, Jerusalem is a "source of lifelong inspiration and career path." As a junior year abroad student at the American College in Jerusalem in the late 1960s, he developed a spiritual and personal connection with the Holy City. Frequenting the Western Wall, he writes poetically of sitting next to the huge Herodian stones, feeling the breeze on his face, and pretending to hear the voices of his ancestors from centuries, even millennia, ago. Decades of advocacy and commitment as senior vice president and lead professional on Israel and other international issues for the New York-based Jewish Council for Public Affairs, Raffel still feels embraced by Jerusalem. It is this knowledge, this love, that he wishes to pass on to his granddaughter, to future generations.

Yes, each of us has moral and practical responsibilities toward ourselves, toward others, including future generations, and toward our environment. The contributors to this book make this clear by sharing important stories and lessons relating not only to themselves, but also to how Jerusalem is special for Judaism, the Jewish people, and Israel. They do so without diminishing Jerusalem's significance to the other inhabitants, principally the Palestinian people, and their needs as well as without ignoring the internal divisions within Jewish Israeli society and relations with the Palestinians.

Jerusalem becomes a true home for all when it fulfills its values of faith, peace, justice, equality, inclusion, reconciliation, and cultural heritage. Jews, Christians, and Muslims, Jewish Israelis and Palestinians, and others are strongly urged to advance the city's inherent goodness and sacredness and care for it as humanity's gift.

This book would not be possible without the generous contributions of the sixteen Jewish authors. My heartfelt thanks are also extended to Dr. Yael S. Aronoff, Dr. Aleen Bayard, Rabbi Marc Aaron Kline, Rabbi Ron Kronish, Dr. Yehezkel Landau, and Mr. Martin J. Raffel for suggesting potential authors; Mr. Rateb Y. Rabie for his guidance and support; and Mr. Elias G. Saboura of Holy Land Books for his assistance and encouragement over the years. This book was supported, in part, by a Creativity and Research Grant from Monmouth University, which is gratefully acknowledged.

1.
Jerusalem: My Favorite City in the World!
Yael S. Aronoff

Jewish Connections to Jerusalem Through the Lens of Personal Connections to Jerusalem

Jerusalem, to Jews in Israel and across the world, is the most holy city. According to the Torah, Josephus, as well as modern scholarship and archeology, King David took over what was a small Canaanite town in the ninth century BCE and made it the capital of his kingdom. King Solomon, King David's son, built the first Temple on Mount Moriah, the site where tradition has it that Abraham was willing to sacrifice his son Isaak. The Temple stood for 410 years before it was destroyed by Nebuchadnezzar of Babylon. The Second Holy Temple was completed by Ezra, Nehemiah, and the returnees from the Babylonian exile in 350 BCE; it stood for 420 years until, in 70 CE, it was destroyed by the governor Titus and the Roman legions.[1]

In the innermost chamber of the first and second Temples, in the Holy of Holies, was the Holy Ark. In the second Temple period, hundreds of thousands of Jews would make pilgrimages to Jerusalem three times a year—for Passover, Shavuot, and Sukkot.[2] After the Temple was twice destroyed, the presence

---

1. Flavius Josephus, *The Jewish Wars* (Oxford University Press, 2017); Hershel Shanks, *The Mystery and the Meaning of the Dead Sea Scrolls* (Cambridge: Harvard University Press, 1997); Frederick E. Greenspahn, *Early Judaism: New Insights and Scholarship* (New York: NYU Press, 2018).

2. Michael Zank, "Jerusalem in Religious Studies," in *Jerusalem: Conflict and Cooperation in a Contested City*, ed. Madelaine Adelman and Miriam Fendius Elman (Syracuse: Syracuse University Press, 2014), p. 139.

of the divine indwelling or *shekhinah* was thought to remain in the ruins, and thus Jews yearned to be as close as possible to where G-d's sacred name could be called upon.[3] It is for this reason that synagogues are built facing the East, facing Jerusalem.

Thus Jerusalem, the site of the destroyed Temple, has been the focus around which Jewish ritual and thought have centered for 2000 years. Over 150,000 Jews are buried on the Mount of Olives, across the valley from the Temple Mount (as the remaining platform upon which the Temple once stood is now known), partly due to the tradition stating that when the Messiah comes, resurrection will start there. For over 700 years, Jewish weddings have included the breaking of the glass, so that even on the happiest of days Jews will remember the destruction of the Temple. This also carries out the vow in the book of Psalms: "If I forget thee, Oh Jerusalem, let my right hand wither, let my tongue stick to my palate if I do not remember you, if I do not set Jerusalem above my greatest joy" (Psalm 137). Many of the Jewish holidays are expressions of yearning for the return to Jerusalem and lament the destruction of the Temples. At the end of Passover seder and at the conclusion of Yom Kippur, Jews say "*L'shanah haba'ah b'Yerushalayim*—Next year in Jerusalem." On *Tisha B'Av*, the Ninth of Av, many Jews mourn the destruction of both Temples, and go to synagogue to read the Book of Lamentations. Religious Jews pray three times a day facing Jerusalem and recite this prayer: "Return to Your city Jerusalem in mercy and establish Yourself there as you promised…Blessed are you, Lord, builder of Jerusalem."

During the Crusades, Jews and Muslims fought together, but were unsuccessful and were expelled from the city. In 1265, Rabbi Nachmanides (Moses Ben Nachman) arrived

---

3. Zank, p. 117.

from Spain and established a synagogue that still exists in Jerusalem, around which the Jewish Quarter grew.

While the significance of Jerusalem to the Jewish religion, to the history of the Jewish people, and to contemporary Jewish life, cannot be overstated, it is certainly too long and complex to capture in a short essay. This, then, will not attempt to be any comprehensive look at the deep history, complex present, and tragic conflicts that entangle the city. Instead, I was invited to reflect on what Jerusalem means to me personally, as well as to Jews as a people. My associations with and reflections on the city will be one thread in a tapestry, and through that tapestry of personal reflections one might attain a broader view of what Jerusalem means to a variety of diverse Jews.

Jerusalem is, simply put, my favorite city in the world. While shaped by religious and historical ties, my own attachment to Jerusalem can best be described as a sense of "secular sacredness"—a sense of the special quality of life in Jerusalem, made up of my experience of and memories of the vibrant life being lived there here and now, but shot through and suffused with the aura of the centuries of Jewish life that still permeates the city. As I ride up the hills from the direction of Tel Aviv, I always feel a sense of anticipation and elation— an anticipation that echoes, in a personal register, the concept of *aliyah*, of "going up" to the city, physically and spiritually, which Israelis now attach to the process of coming to the State of Israel as a whole. I love the ancient Jewish history that is embedded there; I love the current Jewish life that is there (mainly in West Jerusalem within the pre-1967 borders); I love that the city is so important to all three monotheistic religions, that it is diverse and multicultural, that millions of people throughout the world visit it. I love the Jerusalem limestone buildings, I love the vegetation, I love the layers of history, and I love walking every inch of it. My soul feels free in Jerusalem; I feel at home there.

This sense of home might seem surprising, given that I lived there only a total of three years, starting with a year as a young person. I spent much of my early youth growing up in Herzliyah, a town south of Tel Aviv on the Mediterranean. Our family then moved to New Jersey, but we returned to live in Jerusalem during my dad's sabbatical in 1992-1993. I was a first-year student in The Gymnasia Haivrit, a top Israeli high school in the Rehavia neighborhood in West Jerusalem. It was founded in 1909 in Jerusalem's Bukharan neighborhood and moved to the location in Rehavia in 1929. As Arieh Saposnik eloquently writes, discussing the establishment of Jerusalem's Bezalel art school and museum in 1906, these efforts led to a "series of reconceptualizations that ultimately blur the distinctions between the sacred and the secular."[4] We also lived in Rahavia. We did not have a car that year, but I felt a sense of great liberation living in Jerusalem: in contrast to the New Jersey suburbs, where one needed to be driven everywhere, one could walk everywhere in Jerusalem, and we did. Our family probably joined every available educational walk to almost every corner of Jerusalem. I was also on the cross-country team and ran every day through many of Jerusalem's neighborhoods and hills. Throughout that year, I developed a deep connection to Jerusalem's geography, vegetation, diverse peoples, and multi-layered history. I loved running through the different neighborhoods and parks, each with its own character, yet united by the beautiful limestone buildings everywhere. We walked every inch of the Old City: along the top of the old Ottoman wall and on the roofs of houses, through its many alleys. Hearing the many church bells pealing, and the Muslim calls to prayer beautifully echoing across the valleys, and knowing the deep, continuing meaning for the Jewish religion

---

4. Arieh Saposnik, "Changing Faces of Zionism's Jerusalems," in *Jerusalem: Conflict and Cooperation in a Contested City,* ed. Madelaine Adelman and Miriam Fendius Elman (Syracuse: Syracuse University Press, 2014), p. 195.

and history…it is so moving to be grounded in a place that has so many layers of different peoples' histories, including deep meaning for Jewish history, and to make your own history there as well.

Archeologists continually find Jewish history in so many places in Israel, including in Jerusalem. Of the 13 subjects taught each year in the Gymnasia, one was the Bible. It was not taught as a religious text, but as a historical text with which one could and should argue. For example, we discussed what environmental conditions at the time might have contributed to the "parting of the sea" when Moses fled with the Israelites to escape slavery in Egypt to Israel. This way of teaching the Torah in secular schools in Israel—as a non-literal, broad history of the Jewish people grounded in the actual geography of Jerusalem and Israel more broadly—is made "alive" by the constant archeological discoveries that back up this view. Just as I am writing this chapter, 2,731-year-old inscriptions thought to have been authorized by the eighth century BCE Judean King Hezekiah have been discovered in the Siloam Tunnel in the City of David and seem to represent the earliest manuscripts of the Bible.[5] I am moved by the way I can touch that history. I wear a necklace with an authentic ancient Jewish coin found in archeological digs around Israel, dating back to 132-135 CE, minted by Jewish rebels during the third and final revolt against the Romans. On one side, a palm tree; on the other, an inscription calling for the redemption of Jerusalem.

While I believe that G-d is everywhere, and feel especially closer to G-d when contemplating nature, it is also special to put one's hands on the Western Wall—the 2000-year-old retaining wall of the Temple Mount—see the doves often perched in its masonry seams, say a few prayers (always including a prayer for peace in Jerusalem), and write some prayers on paper

5. Judy Siegel-Itzkovich, "Was Proof of Biblical Kings of Israel, Judah Deciphered on Jerusalem Rock Inscriptions?" *Jerusalem Post*, December 28, 2022.

and put them into the cracks. One can feel a deep historical connection to the place itself, and its sacredness. I witness the many people praying fervently at the wall, with some crying as they pray. They include Jews (and non-Jews) from all over the world, as well as many Jewish Israelis who come there regularly to pray. As the Orthodox and ultra-Orthodox have the most influence over the governance of the site, it is segregated by gender, and the men have a much larger section. On top of that, the ultra-Orthodox do not want to be distracted by the singing and praying of women, who are therefore supposed to do so very softly. This has given rise to a movement in Israel, which I fully support, to provide for integrated prayer, whereby women can pray as they like at a section of the wall. I have also thoroughly enjoyed going to the many beautiful churches and mosques in Jerusalem, from which prayers rise just as fervently.

The connection between my classmates, largely from secular or traditional families, was not necessarily a primarily religious one, but rather a historical, cultural, ethnic, and national one that was also infused by a sense of pride and belonging to the city. We took bus rides for a week-long field trip that included many great hikes across the country, and in the bus, everyone would sing, "*Yerushalayim, anachnu me Yerushalayim, anachnu Yerushalmim, Hashir shelanu rak matchil...*" This refrain—"Jerusalem, we are from Jerusalem, we are Jerusalemites, our song has just begun!"—was repeated with enthusiasm and joy. I had classmates whose families had lived in Jerusalem for many generations, and others who were second- or third-generation Israelis whose families came from Yemen, Morocco, and Egypt, as well as a variety of different European countries. One of my classmates and friends was the son of Aharon Appelfeld, a famous Israeli novelist who was a Holocaust survivor. Other famous Israeli novelists who have attended this school include Amos Oz and A.B. Yehoshua, the former President of Israel's Supreme Court, Miriam Naor, and former Israeli Presidents Ephraim Katzir and Reuven Rivlin.

In 1996-1997, my husband and I lived in Jerusalem once again while we were graduate students and I was a Lady Davis Fellow at the Hebrew University, conducting research on the political psychology of Israeli prime ministers for my dissertation research. This time we lived in the German Colony neighborhood and walked almost every inch of the city, having no car. The political context was quite different from that of my childhood memories: Prime Minister Benjamin Netanyahu had come to power in 1996 by the thinnest of margins—29,457 votes—helped by the waves of suicide bombings during the Oslo process, and then especially by a spike in suicide bombings against Israeli civilians near the election, partially motivated by the desire to destroy the peace process promoted by Shimon Peres and his Labor Party. Hamas was opposed to (and officially still opposes) the Oslo Accords, to direct negotiations with Israel, and to a two-state solution.[6] Rather than having Peres carry through Israel's commitments to Oslo, the late 1990s saw Netanyahu try to delay and obstruct the process, claiming that he would carry out Israel's commitments only if the Palestinian Authority upheld its own. Part of Netanyahu's plan to obstruct the future establishment of a Palestinian capital of al-Quds in East Jerusalem was building new Jewish neighborhoods in East Jerusalem, such as Har Homa (between Jerusalem and Bethlehem). My husband and I joined Peace Now protests against the building of this settlement and lamented the spoiling of the initial period of post-Oslo hope at the hands of Hamas, Netanyahu, and new settlers in the West Bank.

We have made many additional trips to Jerusalem since then, including one with our 4-month-old baby in summer

6. Beverly Milton-Edwards & Stephen Farrell, *Hamas* (Cambridge: Polity Press, 2010), p. 81.

1998 to conduct research interviews, as well as the leadership of study abroad programs at the Hebrew University in 2007, 2010, 2013, and 2017. I love to share my love of Jerusalem with my students, Jewish and non-Jewish alike. During each trip, I intentionally live in a different neighborhood of Jerusalem, to savor its variety, and enjoy bringing the students to different neighborhoods to speak to the residents. They converse also with analysts and academics in various think tanks, research centers, and universities, as well as leaders of NGOs and political parties. They have seen heated debates in the Knesset, court sessions in the High Court, and stimulating discussions at the Israel Democracy Institute and at the Truman Center for Peace. They have met with leaders of Peace Now and with the Parents Circle, a group composed of Israelis and Palestinians who have lost relatives to the conflict and who send their children to common summer camps, call each other "brother" and "sister," and speak at each other's schools to fight against demonization. Guided by archeologists, my students also can step through the many layers of Jerusalem's history and its many religious sites.

Communities Living Alongside One Another
One of the things I love most about Jerusalem is the great diversity of cultures, subcultures, religions, and nations. These are at times a source of celebration, but also are infused with cleavages, tensions, and sadness.

One such tension is between ultra-Orthodox Jews on the one hand, and secular and traditional Jews on the other. There are some mutual implicit and explicit biases among the communities. The secular/traditional Jews often feel as if they have a "live and let live" attitude, but believe the ultra-Orthodox want to impinge on the freedom of secular Jews to live as they wish. In polls, 70 percent of secular Jews said they are worried that they will be unable to maintain their preferred lifestyle because of the increasing power of certain other groups in Israeli society; that concern was shared by only 46.5 percent of those defined as traditional with a non-religious tendency, 34 percent of traditional Jews with a religious tendency, 22 percent of national religious and 19 percent of ultra-Orthodox.[7] In Jerusalem, this means there is no public transportation on Shabbat, most of the restaurants are closed, and at times if cars go through an ultra-Orthodox neighborhood, they risk getting stones thrown at them for violating religious laws against driving on Shabbat. As the ultra-Orthodox have many more children, they also have expanded the Jerusalem neighborhoods in which they live, leading some secular/traditional Jews to feel this infringement on their freedoms, and causing some to move to other cities such as Tel Aviv. There is also the resentment of their tax dollars going to the large ultra-Orthodox families when most of the males do not work outside the home but dedicate themselves to the study of the Torah, and of the fact that most ultra-Orthodox men do not serve in the military.

The biases go both ways. Even in high school I remember students applying the derogatory term of "Dossim" to the ultra-Orthodox, and some even muttering something like that under their breath as they passed. However, when I was young and my grandparents came to visit, they made the mistake of sitting next to each other to eat on a stoop in Me'a She'arim, and had hot water thrown on them. Likewise, one summer, when we took our young kids to a playground that was adjacent to an ultra-Orthodox neighborhood, one of the kids spat at them and all the mothers looked disapprovingly at us, as if we might pollute their world by encroaching on it.

---

7. Tamar Hermann and Or Anabi, "Majority Think Too Many Concessions Made to Coalition Partners," Israeli Democracy Institute Israeli Voice Index, January 4, 2023, https://en.idi.org.il/articles/47050.

Despite my own secularism, and my mild resentment of the ultra-Orthodox dictating through their influence things like no public transportation in Jerusalem on Shabbat, I thoroughly enjoy the feeling of Shabbat in Jerusalem. The city is clothed in a quiet, special aura, with far fewer cars and buses; families walk the city, getting together, and many going to synagogue. It produces a special, and even sacred, feeling of peace, making the day a real break from the ordinary routine. The shops close early on Friday, and people bustle about to do their shopping before Shabbat. Going to places like Mahane Yehudah, an outdoor market dominated by Mizrahi Israelis (Jewish Israelis from across the Middle East, North Africa, and Central Asia), is a special experience. It is wonderful to taste and pick one's olives, choose from among the wide selections of Halva, and enjoy the chats and atmosphere.

Another obvious cleavage is that between Palestinians and Jewish Israelis in the city, who largely live in different neighborhoods. The Palestinian and Jewish Israeli identities intersect with day-to-day political realities in ways that make the tangle even denser and more complex. Palestinians living in East Jerusalem currently have ID cards that allow them to work in Israel, but most have rejected the option to take Israeli citizenship as legitimizing Israeli rule. Over time, Israel also made it increasingly difficult to attain Israeli citizenship for those who elected to have it. Many Palestinians have also boycotted municipal elections, thus causing negative influences on day-to-day services in Palestinian neighborhoods. However, many do want to vote for elections that the Palestinian Authority will hold in the future. From 2000 to 2005, over 1,000 Israelis were killed in the Second Intifada, two thirds of whom were civilians. Many buses and restaurants, including a cafeteria at the Hebrew University, were blown up in Jerusalem. Almost every Israeli knows someone who was killed or injured during this time. I, too, have good friends who witnessed a bus being blown up, and who had friends killed. These streets, so peaceful to walk along on Shabbat, also had hundreds of pieces of flesh strewn across them.[8] It is this experience that led Israel to build the "separation barrier"—what my kids called "the sad wall"—that now scars the hills around Jerusalem, separating parts of East Jerusalem from the Old City and West Jerusalem. While popular among many Jewish Israelis because of its perceived success in significantly reducing threats to personal safety and deemed by the International Criminal Court as legal *if* built on the 1967 border, the barrier in fact was built, due to the political influences of certain parties, to encroach on almost 10 percent of the West Bank, and also impinge on Palestinian mobility.

Despite these very real tensions, inequalities, and cleavages that permeate Jerusalem, we live in a world that is not always "either/or" and which encompasses many divergent trends. Jerusalem is certainly not unique in having spaces that are de facto segregated, as well as other spaces in which populations integrate. Jerusalem has vibrant spaces along the "seam" between West and East Jerusalem, around the Old City, where the different subcultures and populations of the city rub up against one another and enjoy the pleasures of a sunny afternoon together. At the outdoor Mamila Mall, for instance, just outside the Jaffa Gate, one can enjoy walking among the shops and listening to performances of street musicians, enjoyed by an audience of secular Jewish Israelis, ultra-Orthodox Jewish

---

8. Those targeting civilians in Israel were mostly not residents of East Jerusalem. This chapter and book focus on Jewish connections to Jerusalem (after Dr. Saliba Sarsar edited similar books on Muslim and on Christian connections to Jerusalem). Every Palestinian also knows someone who has been killed over the decades of conflict with Israel. In the Second Intifada alone, over 3,100 Palestinians were killed, at least 50 percent of whom, by the most conservative estimates, were civilians. (The proportion of civilian casualties, of course, is the subject of intense debate, turning on how different organizations and institutions define "civilian." My point here is not to decide that question, but to acknowledge the pain shared by all in this conflict.)

Israelis, and Palestinian residents of Jerusalem, all shopping together and eating together in the restaurants. Families picnic side by side in the Gan Hapa'amon near Yemin Moshe; children play alongside and with each other in the parks and fountains that run along the Hinnom Valley outside the Old City walls. Jerusalem's trams are used by all and travel to different parts of the city. It is also a city where many people do learn to live alongside one another with tolerance and sometimes form bridges and interactions. There are tensions and extremism of varying ilks, but many families want to live harmoniously with one another.

Jerusalem's Future

The deep connection of Jews to Jerusalem is matched only by the often-negative results for Jews that historically have occurred when others have controlled the city—executions, expulsions, and destruction of Jewish holy sites. For example, in the Byzantine period, Jews were banished from residing in the city.[9] From 1948 to 1967, when it controlled the Old City, Jordan destroyed the Jewish Quarter and would not allow any Jew (Israeli or from anywhere else in the world) to pray at the Western Wall. It also failed to meet the requirements of the 1948 armistice, which provided for free access to the Western Wall and to the Jewish cemeteries and tombs on the Mount of Olives.[10] This history of exclusion and restriction from holy sites is ingrained in Israelis, coloring their attitudes toward sovereignty over the city and anxiety over sharing that space or territory. However, I strongly believe that most of East Jerusalem should be conceded to a Palestinian state in order

---

9. Zank, p. 139.

10. Roger Friedland and Richard D. Hecht, "Sacred Urbanism: Jerusalem's Sacrality, Urban Sociology, and the History of Religions," in *Jerusalem: Conflict and Cooperation in a Contested City,* ed. Madelaine Adelman and Miriam Fendius Elman (Syracuse: Syracuse University Press, 2014), p. 106.

to reach a peace agreement based on a two-state solution. Both Jews and Palestinians deserve to exercise the right to self-determination, and most of East Jerusalem has Palestinian residents, who currently live in a liminal status. While the Temple was twice destroyed, the fact is that now two beautiful mosques exist on that site, and the Muslim *waqf* has religious jurisdiction over the site. As the third holiest Muslim site, it plays an important religious and symbolic role for Palestinians and for a future Palestinian state.

Conceding most of East Jerusalem is difficult for many Jews. Many religious Jews believe that "David's Tunnels" in the Palestinian village of Silwan next to the Old City should remain in Israel's control, as well as the Temple Mount, as it still is holy to Jews. Many religious, as well as some secular, Jews worry that they might be targeted with more violence if Israel cedes control. For instance, there have been many instances of rocks being thrown from the Temple Mount upon Jews praying at the Western Wall below it. If Palestine were to have political sovereignty over the Temple Mount, many would feel that there would be a great security risk, especially if Hamas were ever to be in control.

However, Palestinians are suffering and deserve their own state, with a capital in Jerusalem/*al Quds*. While there will be security risks, the long-term security risks of *not* reaching a peace agreement are much greater. Former President Bill Clinton suggested, in 2000, a creative and helpful set of ideas for getting to such an agreement, known as the "Clinton Parameters." This entailed Israel making the painful compromise of conceding most of East Jerusalem (while retaining the Jewish quarter of the Old City with the Western Wall, as well as some Jewish neighborhoods in East Jerusalem that have existed for over a century), while Palestinians make the painful compromise of limiting the "right of return" for Palestinian refugees to mean de facto the "right of return" largely to the new Palestinian state, with only a limited number being allowed to return to reside in Israel's pre-1967 borders. In that sense, there would be a territorial boundary set based on the 1967 borders, with a swap of any territory Israel kept in East Jerusalem, for territory in pre-1967 Israel that would become part of Palestine; similarly, the two most emotional issues tied to identities would essentially largely be swapped for one other.[11]

Attitudes of Israelis toward such sharing of the city varies widely, depending on how the questions are phrased. If they are phrased in terms of "dividing the city" that has already been "united" under Israeli sovereignty, then some surveys show that many Jewish Israelis would be reluctant to concede most of East Jerusalem. However, far more are willing to make this concession if the survey questions are phrased as "conceding Palestinian villages" to which most Jewish Israelis never go in the first place. In that sense, if the question is posed as acknowledging the sharing of a city that is already largely segregated and divided, far more Israelis are willing to make this concession for peace. In 2017, a survey also showed that 61 percent of Jews and 54 percent of Arabs agreed with the statement that, "at present Jerusalem is actually divided into two cities: the eastern city and the western city."[12] These results are explained by prospect theory in psychology, which finds that people put a higher value on items that they consider to be "theirs" and therefore would pose a "loss," than they place on "gains." In late 2017, in answer to the question "Should

11. Daniel C. Kurtzer and Scott B. Lasensky with William B. Quandt, Steven L. Spiegel, and Shibley I. Telhami, *Negotiating Arab-Israeli Peace: American Leadership in the Middle East* (Washington, D.C.: United States Institute of Peace Press, 2008), pp. 145-157.

12. "'62% of Jewish Public Holding onto Territories in Judea, Samaria Not an Occupation:' 50 Years on, monthly Peace Index focuses on anniversary of the Six Day War," Israel Democracy Institute, June 4, 2017, https://en.idi.org.il/press releases/15728. *The Peace Index is a project of the Evens Program for Mediation and Conflict Resolution at Tel Aviv University and the Guttman Center for Public Opinion and Policy Research of the Israel Democracy Institute.*

Israel, as part of a settlement that would end the conflict with the Palestinians, transfer the rule of the Arab neighborhoods in East Jerusalem to the Palestinians, or should it continue to control them, even at the cost of a settlement that would end the conflict?" 51 percent of respondents said they would prefer to transfer the rule of East Jerusalem's Arab neighborhoods to Palestinian control; only 49 percent said they would prefer to retain them.[13]

I always feel Jerusalem calling me to it, and I feel deeply bonded to it. I return to it almost every year, always feeling a pull to stay when I leave. However, my close family does not live there so it is unlikely that I will. It is up to Israelis and Palestinians living there to find a way to divide/share it that will enable both peoples to live in peace and equality.

Some creative solutions have been proposed over the years. Ehud Olmert, in 2008, offered most of East Jerusalem to be established as the Palestinian capital al-Quds; in exchange for Israel's retention of the Jewish quarter of the Old City and Jewish neighborhoods in East Jerusalem, he offered to swap pre-1967 territory in Israel. In that scenario, it was envisioned that the Old City would be jointly administered by the U.S., Israel, Palestine, Jordan, the EU, and Saudi Arabia.[14] There have been many creative ideas for dividing and sharing Jerusalem, including that of Al-Quds and Yerushalayim being respective capitals of two fully independent sovereign states, but with mechanisms for coordination within the context of confederation. In this formula, if Israel kept all the Jewish neighborhoods within Jerusalem's current municipal

---

13. Zipi Israeli and Udi Dekel, "The Future of Jerusalem: Between Public Opinion and Policy," Tel Aviv University's Institute for National Security Studies, INSS Insight No. 1057, May 15, 2018.

14. David Ignatius, "The Mideast Deal that Could Have Been," *Washington Post*, October 26, 2011.

boundaries, Al-Quds would be able to expand alongside the municipal boundaries of Yerushalayim.[15]

Surveys of Israeli and Palestinian public opinion provide hope that future scenarios for dividing/sharing Jerusalem could find support. When leaders reach a peace agreement that makes Israeli and Palestinian constituencies confident that Palestinian independence and peace will be secured, it is likely that support for compromise and accommodation will grow. In June 2022, a survey showed that half (48%) of Jerusalem's Palestinian residents said that they would prefer to become citizens of Israel, while 43 percent would choose to be a citizen of Palestine, and 9 percent would choose Jordanian citizenship. Around half (54%) of East Jerusalem's Palestinians agree with the statement, "I hope someday we can be friends with Israelis, since we are all human beings after all." Surveys show that most of the Jewish Israeli public (65%) feels that Israel should not allow any—or only limited—Jewish ascent to the Temple Mount/Haram al Sharif. By contrast, 35 percent of that same public favors allowing Jews to visit and pray freely on the Temple Mount. The surveys also indicate that at times of security tensions, public support for Jewish freedom to visit the Temple Mount—in particular, visits by high profile public officials—drops dramatically, compared to times of relative peace.[16] These surveys show a willingness on the part

---

15. Hiba Husseini and Yossi Beilin, eds., *The Holy Land Confederation as a Facilitator of the Two State Solution,* pp. 53-60. Unfortunately, the Israeli government formed in December 2022 is the most right-wing government in Israel's history, and opposes conceding any part of East Jerusalem, and opposes a two-state solution. It is likely that future governments will have to concede most of East Jerusalem for peace.

16. David Pollock, "New Poll Reveals Moderate Trend Among East Jerusalem Palestinians," Washington Institute for Near East Policy Fikra Forum, July 8, 2022. Poll conducted in June 2022 by the Palestine Center for Public Opinion and commissioned by the Washington Institute for Near East Policy.

of most Israelis to prioritize peace above the right to pray at the Temple Mount.

These surveys show that there is hope for reaching a division/sharing of Jerusalem in a future two-state solution. Such a scenario would continue to enable Jews to implement their deepest connections to Jerusalem, while also exercising Jewish (and universal) values that would support self-determination for Palestinians as well as Jews.

Next year in Jerusalem, in peace for all.

2.

Next Year in Jerusalem: When Aspiration Meets Reality
Naamah Kelman

The Jewish liturgical canon is full of references to Jerusalem. Jerusalem appears in many prayers and blessings. There is not one prayer service or major lifecycle ritual that does not mention Jerusalem. This includes the daily prayers, the Blessing after a meal, major and minor holiday prayers. References to Jerusalem are included in the blessings at weddings, as are words of comfort for mourners. When Jews pray, they face Jerusalem.

All these rituals begin to evolve after the fall of the Second Temple in 70 CE. Once Jerusalem and the Temple are lost to Jewish control, and the dispersion of Jewish communities accelerates, the yearning for the return to Temple worship, along with the hope of a return to Jerusalem, intensifies. There are blessings, prayers, and rituals that express the idea of remembering Jerusalem. This is most vividly presented in the wedding ritual.

Every Jewish wedding includes this blessing:

> *Praised be God, Who created joy and gladness, groom and bride, mirth, glad song, pleasure, delight, love, brotherhood, peace, and companionship. Eternal, our God, let there soon be heard in the cities of Judah and **the streets of Jerusalem** the sound of joy and the sound of gladness, the voice of the groom and the voice of the bride, the sound of the grooms' jubilation from their wedding canopies and of the*

*youths from their song-filled feasts. Praised are You
Who gladdens the groom with the bride.*

This is a nostalgic longing for what once was. In fact, the final blessing recited at the end of the ceremony recalls the voices of bride and groom, as they raised them in the archways and walkways of Jerusalem.

In addition, the breaking of a glass object is considered the climax of the wedding ceremony. This act has different origins than those of its current understanding. Originally, broken jugs were meant to scare away demons from the young couple as they went home after the wedding. Over time, the ceramics turned to glass and the meaning became associated with loss, specifically the loss of Jerusalem.[17] In a traditional ceremony, the groom will recite a passage from Psalms 137:5-7. The words are as follows (a paraphrase rather than an exact translation):

> If I forget you, O Jerusalem, let my right hand forget her cunning, let my tongue cleave to the roof of my mouth, if I forget you, as I must set Jerusalem as my greatest joy.

At our greatest moment of family and community joy and hope, Jerusalem is restored as the grand coda of the ceremony. Our joy cannot be complete without longing for Jerusalem, perhaps remembering a future restored Jerusalem, including the re-establishment of the Temple.

The passage from Psalm 137, "if I forget thee, O Jerusalem," evolved from longing for Jerusalem to something more aspirational, more directed to actual return to Jerusalem. In addition to the longing, a significant pronouncement was added to two major festivals. As if the longing were not enough, a tradition evolved that we make a collective declaration to affirm a return to Jerusalem. This is the Jerusalem reference that I chose to focus on: **"Next Year in Jerusalem."** It appears twice

---

17. Jacob Z. Lauterbach, "The Ceremony of the Breaking of the Glass at Weddings," *Hebrew Union College Annual,* Vol. 2 (1925): 351-80.

a year, in both cases at the end of important Jewish moments. The first is at the end of the Yom Kippur (Day of Atonement) Service, and the second is at the end of the Passover Seder.

The liturgy and calendar of the Jewish People are rooted in the Land of Israel with Jerusalem at its heart. The two most significant days of the Hebrew Calendar are Yom Kippur (Day of Atonement) and Passover. Both are based in the Hebrew Bible, and both involve elaborate rituals and prayer, although they are two very distinct components of the Jewish faith.

Yom Kippur is a day of fasting and collective prayer, a personal day of atonement when the individual is focusing on repentance and restoration. It is considered the holiest day of the year, when we have asked for forgiveness, have made amends with our fellows, and now face God. Much of the liturgy includes lists of our collective sins. Yet, we conclude with a prayer of hope for the entire people. The very last words we chant at the end of our many hours of prayer and fasting are: "Next Year in Jerusalem!"

Similarly, references to Jerusalem can be found throughout the Passover Seder, which is probably the oldest continuous ritual of the Jewish people. Starting in Biblical times and evolving over centuries, much was added and subtracted to this ritual. Passover is a reminder of the collective story of the exodus from Egypt and the formation of the Jewish People, which includes a loose retelling of the Biblical story of the Exodus from Egypt and eating very specific foods. This most joyful ritual also concludes with the words: "Next Year in Jerusalem!"

Throughout history, Jews around the world—from Poland to Yemen, from Iraq to London and to the United States—stood up at the end of these two momentous events and exclaimed this sentence: "Next Year in Jerusalem!" One might say these twin declarations serve as two pillars that hold up these mirror holidays, some six months apart from each other. Yom Kippur is devoted to the individual Jew seeking redemption, in the context of the collective, whereas the Passover Seder, part of the longer seven-day holiday celebrating our collective Redemption, is held in the context of the family. Nevertheless, both conclude with the same stirring words.

Why do these words appear as the coda for the two rituals? In both cases, they express the aspiration for "messianic Redemption."

The phrase "next year in Jerusalem" appears in the liturgy in the tenth century. It is assumed that it was taken from liturgical poems (Piyutim) that appear in different Jewish communities. Some of these liturgical poems are later integrated into the prayerbook, and this specific saying has found its way into the two fundamental rituals discussed above, serving as the last declarative hope and call.

What does "Next Year in Jerusalem" mean? Is it an aspiration? A messianic hope? A travel plan? A political statement? A desire to celebrate this moment in Jerusalem rather than where the worshipper is currently residing? It is over centuries that Jews chanted these lines and had no clue as to what Jerusalem was in reality. Who was there? What did Jerusalem look like? What was built over the "remains" of the Holy Temple? Who was sovereign over Jerusalem?

Yet, in effect, nobody translated these words into action. Jews stayed where they were for another year, and another year, and if they moved, it was to another Diasporic location. Jewish tradition developed a theological construct that justified the need to refrain from moving to the land of Israel. It was argued that "next year" is only a metaphor for the future and the return to the ancestral land will only happen when the Messiah will come. And the Messiah will come only when God decides and when the people are worthy of redemption.

Modern Zionism changed this construct. "Next Year" could actually literally mean "next year" or, if not that, then in the near future, whenever conditions will allow. Modern Zionism was a mixture of rebellious secular alternative to the religious tradition and new theology that explained why the time has come. Modern Zionism turned this call into an action plan.

As a liberal religious Jew who lives in today's Jerusalem, I wish to address the complex meaning of this prayer / statement and other references to Jerusalem that exist in our tradition. I do so, knowing well what Jerusalem on the ground is like. My Jerusalem is as concrete as it gets; it is part of my daily life.

What comes to my mind when I chant "Next Year..."? Should I stop saying it, given the fact that I am already there? And if I hold on to my tradition and say these words, what do they mean to me? What do other Jews in Israel think about this phrase when they are confronted with it? Similarly, what do Jews around the world who can freely travel to Israel think about when they perform those same rituals? This is complicated, as Jewish people live and thrive in Diaspora communities, and for Israeli Jews, I would venture to say that this declaration has "returned" to its original aspirational meaning. We remain in an imperfect world, and today's longing for Jerusalem represents this imperfect world.

For centuries, Jerusalem included the Church of the Holy Sepulchre and two mosques, the Dome of the Rock and Al-Aqsa Mosque, and the Western Wall, the one remaining segment of the Holy Israelite Temple's Outer Wall. In today's Jerusalem, they stand together in an increasingly fragile reality, and literally on the same spot.

Jerusalem remains a complex and divisive city. No one expresses the dichotomy of this City for Jews better than the modern Hebrew poet, Yehudah Amichai, in his last book of poetry, *Open Closed Open; Poems*:[18]

---

18. Yehuda Amichai, *Open Closed Open; Poems* (New York: Harcourt, Inc., 2000).

Sometimes Jerusalem is a city of knives.
Even the hopes for peace are sharp, to cut through
the hard reality...
Church bells keep trying to ring out a calm round tone;
But they grow heavy, like a pestle in a mortar pounding
artillery shells
The Cantor and the muezzin want to sweeten their tune,
But in the end, a piercing wail cuts through the din:
The Lord God of us all, the Lord God is
One, one, one (Chad!),

And there are days here when everything is sails and more sails,
Even though there's no sea in Jerusalem, not even a river.
Everything is sails: the flags, the prayer shawls, the black coats,
the monks' robes, the kaftans and kaffiyehs,
young women's dresses and headdresses,
Torah mantles and prayer rugs, feelings that swell in the wind
Are sails, all of them sails in the splendid regatta
On the two seas of Jerusalem:
The sea of memory and the sea of forgetting.

These two stanzas from the poem "Jerusalem, Jerusalem, Why Jerusalem?" express the fact that we live both in the Middle East and in the Mediterranean region. There are days when all we hear are sirens, and booms, and ambulances whirling, and then days when we sit at our cafés sipping coffee, enjoying the lovely breezes, where "everything is sails." We experience the endless horizons as well as the vertical posts that hold up the walls and fences that separate.

"Chad" in Hebrew means "ONE" as well as "sharp, cutting." Three religions exist here side by side, each claiming the Oneness, the only-ness of their GOD, or so we live together when we cannot avoid the church bells, the muezzin calling Muslims to prayer, and the siren announcing the Jewish Sabbath.

Walk in the Old City, through the Arab *shuk* (*souk*) and look up. Blowing in the breeze are the Jewish prayer shawls, the Arab dresses, kufiyahs, scarves, and Christian robes, for sale, side by side. Pilgrims from all over the world, Ultra-Orthodox and secular Jews, Christian tourists of all denominations walk the narrow steps leading to church or mosque or to the Wailing Wall and synagogues. But exit any gate, and we return to the mundane of our lives, in our segregated city, where people segregate from each other by ethnicity, language, religious beliefs, and social strata.

If we manage to avoid each other, we can live together.

The realities of Jerusalem were not part of the family Seder nor the liturgy that culminates the end of Yom Kippur. It is only with the rise of Zionism and the return to Jerusalem, and with the establishment of the State of Israel, that Jews began to face the real Jerusalem. Two significant dates have changed the relationship to Jerusalem for Jews. The first is May 1948, when the State of Israel was established but the city was divided, with the Holy places remaining in Jordan. Then in June 1967, when Israel regained control of the Old City, a new connection emerged.

It is not the intention of this essay to explore the political issues of what is a contested, "united" city. Nor do I offer any geo-political insights or analysis that can contribute to a possible resolution.

Are we doomed to live between the poet Amichai's "chad" and the sharp sounds of bullets, bombs, and knives, each claiming a monopoly on the earthly and the heavenly Jerusalem? Or can we all sail on the poet Amichai's regatta of ships gliding freely on the "seas" of Jerusalem, propelled by forgetting and remembering? Are these hopes expressed from the ancient Book of Psalms possible?

From Psalm 122
> A song of ascents. Of David. I rejoiced when they said to me,
> "We are going to the House of God"
>
> Our feet stood inside your gates, O Jerusalem,
>
> Jerusalem built up, a city knit together,
>
> to which tribes would make pilgrimage,
> the tribes of the Holy One
>
> Pray for the well-being of Jerusalem;
> "May those who love you be at peace.
>
> May there be well-being within your ramparts,
> peace in your citadels."

We live in times when divisions and fractures are consuming us, making working together and even simple conversations more challenging and increasingly impossible. This is true in the political climates of the U.S. and Israel. There are moments when Jerusalem offers a faint hope of coexistence. Our Israeli health system is often cited as a model where all residents work together and are treated together. There are important educational projects for shared society, at the institution that I lead.[19] However, more often there are mutual disdain and disconnection.

Until we can all see one another, until we can hear the multiple stories and attachments, we will live in a beautiful but disputed, disjointed city. If we succeed in reaching out to the other, perhaps, like the broken glass that ends each Jewish wedding, we can sweep the pieces together, and fire them once more in a new form, shimmering for all.

---

19. "Advancing Tolerance in Jerusalem: The Teachers' Lounge," http://huc.edu/campus-life/jerusalem/advancing-tolerance-in-jerusalem-teachers-lounge.

3.

What Jerusalem Means to Me
John L. Rosove

Jerusalem is a singularly wondrous place. Yet, it remains a divided city straddling uneasily the fault lines between ultra-Orthodox Haredi Jews and secular-non-Orthodox Jews, and between Israeli Jews and Palestinian Arabs. I wonder if a unified city is possible, though there are many grassroots efforts to try and bridge the chasms among the different religious, cultural, and national identities.

This piece of real estate, which is holy to three great religions, is among the most famous and dysfunctional in the world with its iconic golden dome and ancient wall, where prophets preached, psalmists sang praises, mystics sought oneness with the Divine, sages taught wisdom from ancient texts, and tribes and nations battled for control. This complex ancient and modern city nestled between valleys nevertheless sparks the imagination, passions, and yearnings of billions. I am one of them.

What happens there is, of course, of deep importance to the Jewish people as the center of Judaism, but it is important not only to us. Because the State of Israel rules over all Jerusalem, we who love the city must be sensitive to others who claim her as their own, because Jerusalem belongs to them too.

History ought to be a warning of what can happen if events and passions are not held in check. In its 4000-year life, this so-called "City of Peace" has rarely known peace. It has been attacked 52 times, captured and recaptured 44 times, besieged 23 times, and destroyed twice.

Often I climbed to the roof of the Church of the Holy Sepulchre to see the sweep of the landscape, and I marvel that I can see so much in a glance: Old City streets—Jewish, Christian, Armenian, and Muslim Quarters—the ancient Mount of Olives Jewish cemetery—medieval churches—the Temple Mount and Noble Sanctuary—the Western Wall, Dome of the Rock, and Southern-Most Mosque—Mount Scopus and the Hebrew University—a plethora of embassies and the Intercontinental Hotel—the City of David and the Palestinian village of Silwan—the sloping convergence of the Valley of Hinnom and the Valley of Kidron—the Security Fence—West and East Jerusalem—and the Seam Line.

I love this ancient-modern place. One thousand years ago, the Spanish poet, philosopher, and thinker Yehudah Halevi[20] spoke words that resonate with me: "My heart is in the east and I am at the far reaches of the west."

Among the most inspirational and transcendent moments I experienced in Jerusalem came to me in the days and weeks following the outbreak of the Yom Kippur War in October 1973. I lived in Jerusalem from August of that year to May of the next during my first year of rabbinic study at the Hebrew Union College. During the war, classes were canceled and we students volunteered in a variety of places throughout the city that needed help after young Israeli men were called to fight at the front. I, with twenty others, volunteered to work the nightshift (10:00 pm to 6:00 am) at Jerusalem's Berman Bakery, one of two large bakeries on the outskirts of the city. Each day we produced between 60,000 and 85,000 loaves of bread for the citizens of Jerusalem and soldiers on the Egyptian front.

20. Yehudah Halevi (1071-1141) died mysteriously and shortly after arriving in the Holy Land when it was controlled by Christian Crusaders.

Having walked every night in the blacked-out city during that three-week period to and from my dorm to the volunteer pick-up point, I remember the serene calm and utter quiet in those Jerusalem streets that so belied the ferocity of fighting on the Egyptian and Syrian fronts. Looking to the sky, I felt simple wonder as I beheld thousands of stars, as if tiny lanterns dangled from the black velvet firmament and sparkled in the clear, cold, and moon-less autumn sky. They appeared as a shimmering blanket of light cast lovingly over Jerusalem, offering our people and all peoples protection from injury and harm. It was a glorious sight, and each night it took my breath away.

However, one of my saddest moments as a Jew occurred also in Jerusalem when I served as the national Chair of the Association of Reform Zionists of America.[21] One day, the international leadership of the Reform and Conservative movements and Nashot HaKotel (Women of the Wall)[22] marched with Torah scrolls carried by our leaders into the Kotel Plaza to affirm our right as Jews to pray according to our liberal egalitarian Jewish values and customs at the holiest site in all of Judaism. I followed in the procession immediately behind my friend Anat Hoffman, a well-known and recognizable figure, who is the director and a founding member of Women of the Wall.

Anat wrapped herself lovingly in her tallit and carried one of the Torah scrolls. After passing through security, we hundred-strong Jews from Israel and around the world sang

21. The Association of Reform Zionists of America (ARZA) represents 1.5 million American Reform Jews and is the largest Zionist organization in the United States. I served as the national Chairperson between 2016 and 2018.

22. Women of the Wall (Hebrew: Nashot Hakotel) was formed in 1988 and meets on the first day of every Hebrew month (i.e., Rosh Hodesh). It is a multi-denominational Jewish feminist organization based in Israel whose goal is to secure the rights of women to pray at the Western Wall in a fashion that includes singing, reading aloud from the Torah, and wearing religious garments.

celebratory songs as we entered into the large Western Wall Plaza. Enraged ultra-Orthodox Haredi men and boys verbally and then physically assaulted us because they were offended when they heard the voices of women ("Kol Ishah")[23] singing. Their sensibilities were further disturbed in seeing Jewish women carrying Torah scrolls and preparing with men to pray together in a large egalitarian prayer service in the Plaza. According to the ultra-Orthodox Chief Rabbi of the Wall, Torah scrolls not under his strict supervision are forbidden to be brought from the outside and into the Plaza, and no services were permitted except in designated prayer spaces between the Kotel and a metal barrier fence.

I have an old photograph from the Ottoman period (before 1917) that shows women and men praying alongside one another at this holiest site. Eventually Orthodox rabbis unilaterally took control of and designated the entire area as an ultra-Orthodox "synagogue" overseen by them according to their rules despite that area being an international spiritual center for the entirety of the Jewish people.

Several of us surrounded Anat as we moved forward into the Plaza because we feared for her physical safety. She has been harassed for years by Haredi thugs and was arrested by the police for carrying and reading from an unapproved Torah scroll thus stimulating the ire of ultra-Orthodox Jews. They were not arrested for their disorderly conduct—she was. A classic case of blame-the-victim instead of the aggressor.

Our fears were fulfilled almost immediately when one furious young Haredi man ran toward us and lunged at Anat attempting to tear from her arms the scroll she was carrying.

---

23. "Kol Ishah—The voice of the woman"—the prohibition against men hearing women sing is based on the Babylonian Talmud, Sota 48a: "Rav Yosef said: men singing with women answering [constitutes] immodesty; women singing with men answering is like [setting] fire to sawdust. What is the practical distinction [between the two]? The abolishment of the [latter] should precede the [former]."

Instinctively, I stepped between him and Anat, and like a tackle guarding my quarterback, I blocked him and knocked him to the stone pavement. He was as stunned as I was. I don't know what he felt or thought, but I felt shame that here, of all places, in Jerusalem, at the center of Judaism, at our people's holiest site, I had been forced by him to act violently against a fellow Jew in defense of my friend, and on behalf of the principle of gender equality in Judaism and religious pluralism in the Jewish State as assured in Israel's Declaration of Independence.

On another occasion, I attended a monthly Women of the Wall Rosh Hodesh service at the Kotel. In support of these women's right to pray together at the Western Wall, I stood with several male friends on the other side of the mechitzah (separation fence between women and men) only a meter from where the women were davening at the back of the Ezrat Nashim (the women's section). I strained to hear their voices as they prayed ever-so quietly to avoid offending ultra-Orthodox sensibilities concerning "Kol Ishah."

Standing on a chair near the mechitzah and screaming obscenities at the women, an elderly Jew, surrounded by dozens of like-minded Haredi young men and boys, screamed to drown out the barely audible women's prayer. The women, despite this egregiously insulting attack, continued praying with humility, dignity, and grace.

I thought then of the Talmudic explanation for the destruction of the Second Temple of Jerusalem in 70 C.E.—*sinat chinam*, that is, "gratuitous hatred" of one Jew toward another.[24] That day the hatred flowed in only one direction, from the Haredi men and boys to the worshipping Nashot Hakotel.

It is no secret that we Jews disagree with each other passionately on matters of God, prophecy, faith, ethics, law,

---

24. Babylonian Talmud, Yoma 9b.

authority, power, sovereignty, politics, and Jewish identity. Spirited argument is in our people's DNA. However, the Talmudic sages regarded civility to be so important a virtue that they ruled almost always according to the opinions of Hillel[25] on matters of law and tradition as opposed to the opinions of his opponent Shammai, because Hillel included within his arguments his respectful acknowledgment of Shammai's position.

To know Jerusalem well is a difficult proposition. The city is among the most complex amalgams of faiths, cultures, peoples, and politics in the world. The dynamic of so many forces often leads to misunderstandings and at times to violence.

Daniel Rossing,[26] once the Deputy Mayor of Jerusalem for Interreligious Affairs under Mayor Teddy Kollek,[27] told me a story years ago concerning Jerusalem's Armenian Christian Patriarch Yeghishe Derderian[28] and his confrontation with a survivor of the Holocaust who lived in the Jewish Quarter and very close to the patriarchal residence in the Armenian Quarter of the Old City. One year, during the festival of Sukkot on a Shabbat afternoon following an Armenian Christian celebration in the Church of the Holy Sepulchre, as

---

25. First century B.C.E.

26. Daniel Rossing (1946-2010) was an academic, humanitarian, and philanthropist who founded the Jerusalem Center for Jewish-Christian Relations (JCJCR) in 2004. He was awarded the Mount Zion Award in 2009 in recognition for his contribution to developing dialogue and understanding among Jews, Christians, and Muslims throughout Jerusalem and Israel. See https://rossingcenter.org/about/?five.

27. Mayor Teddy Kollek (1911-2007), born in Hungary, was an Israeli politician who served as the Mayor of Jerusalem from 1965 to 1993.

28. Armenian Patriarch Yeghishe Derderian (1911-1990) lost all of his relatives in 1915 during the Armenian genocide. He arrived in Jerusalem at the age of 12 to study at the St. James Theological Seminary. He served eventually as the dean of the seminary before being named deputy patriarch of Jerusalem in 1949. In 1960, he became the 95th Armenian Patriarch of Jerusalem and served for thirty years until his death in February 1990. See https://www.nytimes.com/1990/02/07/obituaries/yeghishe-derderian-80-armenian-patriarch.html.

he often did with his faithful, Derderian led a procession to his official residence in the Armenian Quarter. With every step he banged his large golden cross upon the stone pavement. As he approached his residence near the Jewish quarter where the Holocaust survivor lived, the survivor of the Holocaust heard him coming and was infuriated to have her Sukkot and Shabbat afternoon rest disturbed once again by the patriarch and his followers. She took a pail of water, and as the Patriarch passed, she dumped the water over his head from the Sukkah on her balcony.

Infuriated and insulted, Derderian called Daniel immediately to complain. Daniel came promptly to Derderian's residence, heard his bitter tale, walked across the way to the woman's apartment, and explained to her how deeply insulted the Armenian Christian Patriarch was by what she had done. She responded: "These Christians stood passively by in Germany while my entire family and I were taken away to the camps. I was the only one who survived. This is my country, and I have had enough of them."

Daniel asked if she knew that between 1915 and 1917 the Armenian community in Turkey too was the victim of a genocide of more than one million murdered by the Ottoman Turks. She did not know. Upon hearing this, her face fell and her affect softened. Daniel asked her to accompany him across the way to meet with Derderian. She agreed. Daniel explained to the Patriarch that this woman was a survivor of the Holocaust and had lost her entire family to the Nazis. His face also fell and his affect too softened. He shared with her that he had lost his entire family in the Armenian genocide and that he, like her, was the only member of his family who survived.

In listening to each other and in coming to know one another's personal experiences, both realized how much they shared. The woman apologized to Derderian. He openheartedly accepted her apology and offered his sympathy for the enormous loss in her family that he knew only too well in his.

Here is another example of opposites finding common ground through civility and listening, though, admittedly, it is a far less dramatic tale than that of the Jewish survivor and the Armenian survivor. In October 2016, I attended a meeting of the Board of Governors of the Jewish Agency for Israel[29] in my role as ARZA Chair and was asked to lobby at the Knesset in a visit to the MK Yehuda Glick, an Orthodox settler and father of five from the Likud Party. I was part of a 100-delegate visit to 27 MKs concerning three issues before the Jewish Agency: religious pluralism, support for the anti-BDS movement, and greater support for aliyah.

MK Yehuda Glick was called "the most dangerous Jew in Israel" because he wanted to establish a synagogue on the Temple Mount. He already had been arrested many times in his attempts to pray there.

Since 1967, the Israeli government, in cooperation with the Muslim Waqf,[30] has agreed that, to keep the peace, no Jewish prayers would be held on the platform the Muslims call "The Noble Sanctuary" and Jews call "The Temple Mount."

In 2014, Glick was shot four times in the chest by a Palestinian Muslim terrorist who, before shooting him, said; "I am sorry—but you are an enemy of Al Aqsa!" Glick's assailant

29. The Jewish Agency for Israel (JAFI - Hebrew: Sochnut) is the largest Jewish non-profit organization in the world. It was established in 1929 as the operative branch of the World Zionist Organization, known as the "Parliament of the Jewish People." JAFI provides the global framework for Aliyah, ensures global Jewish safety, strengthens Jewish identity, connects Jews to Israel and one another, and conveys the voice of the Jewish People to the State of Israel to help shape its society.

30. The Jerusalem Islamic Waqf, founded by the King of Jordan in 1948, is a religious trust that oversees the current Islamic edifices on and around the Temple Mount or al-Haram al-Sharif in the Old City of Jerusalem, including the Al-Aqsa Mosque and the Dome of the Rock.

escaped on a motorcycle and was pursued and killed by Israeli security forces. Though wounded seriously, Yehuda recovered after three months in the hospital.

When we met, I told him how happy I was that he had survived. I introduced myself as the ARZA Chair and explained that I had been a co-chair of the national Rabbinic and Cantorial Cabinet of J Street, two liberal American Zionist organizations supporting a two-state solution to the Israeli-Palestinian conflict. He joked, "Given your background, I'm surprised you're glad I'm alive."

MK Glick shared his vision of a united Jerusalem, a "city of peace," his belief in human rights for all peoples, and his support for religious pluralism in the State of Israel. I was surprised that he, a right-wing Orthodox settler Jew, had voted for the right of Reform and Conservative converts to use state mikvaot (immersion baths) and for the government's plan to build an egalitarian prayer space in the Southern Kotel Plaza beneath Robinson's Arch.

"What difference does it make to me that women want to wear tefillin, that you want to pray at the Kotel according to your practice, and that Reform and Conservative Jews and Women of the Wall want equal rights in Israel—they should have equal rights and be able to pray at the Kotel any way you like in a new prayer space!" he said.

Glick said that Jerusalem should be an example of coexistence and mutual respect, a light to the nations[31] of the world, where the three great faith traditions live peacefully and respectfully side-by-side, willing to share space.

I said, "Yehuda, you realize that if Jews tried to erect a synagogue on the Temple Mount the Muslim world would rise up in revolt and World War III would result?"

---

31. Isaiah 42:6, 49:6, 60:3.

He understood my fears and said, "It's a process, and it will take time."

He believed that the time had passed for a two-state solution. He advocated for one state in which all citizens enjoy equal rights, privileges, government services, resources for education and for their communities, and access to business opportunities and modern living. He said that there ought to be more Arab ministers in the Israeli government.

While I agree that all citizens of the democratic State of Israel must have equal civil rights, I don't agree with Yehuda that there should be one state because one state will result either in Israel losing its democracy by denying equal civil and voting rights to its Palestinian Arab citizens (who might one day become the majority), or in risking the loss of the greatest accomplishment of the Jewish people in two thousand years, the creation of a democratic Jewish and sovereign state in the Land of Israel. I also told him how I worried about the risks his advocacy for a synagogue on the Temple Mount posed. All told, I was stunned by how thoughtful, pluralistic, non-violent, civil, unpredictable, open-hearted, and compassionate a man MK Yehuda Glick is, though he has extreme views for Jerusalem.

We had to end our conversation in order to meet with the Prime Minister and Knesset Speaker. After that meeting ended, Yehuda made a special effort to find me and wish me well.

The most important challenge in Jerusalem, in Israel as a whole, and throughout the Middle East is that people from different religious, cultural, ethnic, and national backgrounds must find a way to understand each other and accept their differences. Dr. Martin Luther King's words ring true in Israel as in the United States: "People don't get along because they fear each other. People fear each other because they don't know each other. They don't know each other because they have not properly communicated with each other."[32]

There are multiple efforts throughout Israel in which Palestinian Arab Israeli citizens and Israeli Jewish citizens meet, talk, listen to one another, and seek common ground. More of that is necessary in order to make peace. In the meantime, the Psalmist's plea ought to be uppermost in our hearts, minds, and souls: *"Sha'alu shalom Yerushalayim—* Pray for the peace of Jerusalem!"[33]

---

32. Rev. Martin Luther King Jr. spoke these words in King Chapel at Cornell College, Mount Vernon, Iowa, on October 15, 1962.

33. Psalm 122:6.

4.
Jerusalem in My Life
Peretz Rodman

I. City of Dreams, City of Dreamers

In mid-September 1973, I flew to Israel for my first visit, to spend a year as a visiting student at the Hebrew University of Jerusalem. After a stop at the apartment rented for three of us by a friend who had arrived a month earlier, my flat mates and I set out to explore the central shopping and business district of (Jewish west) Jerusalem. I was surprised to find such contemporary Western phenomena as pizzerias and ice cream shops, delighted to have my first taste of falafel, and enchanted by the ubiquitous presence of Hebrew, written and spoken all around me.

As we passed Independence Park, we were approached by a wiry, energetic older man—so it seemed, although he was much younger than I am today—who, although dressed in a slapdash, almost shabby fashion, carried himself and spoke like someone on a crucial and urgent mission. In rapid-fire Hebrew he told us his name and his title: Coordinator of World Peace in Jerusalem. Yes, he continued without waiting a moment for us to inquire, had it not been foretold by the prophet Isaiah that the nations would come together here in Yerushalayim to bring about an accord that would see the end of war and bloodshed, peace flowing like a mighty river? He was the one whose task was to make this happen. He was striving to bring together representatives of all the nations of the world to negotiate a new world order of universal peace.

To underscore his claim, he produced from his pocket a gently tattered business card confirming his name and his impressive title, briefly held it out for us to see, and snatched it back to be preserved. It was clearly the only one of its kind. He scurried off without a word of inquiry about us, his interlocutors. That, we understood, was not a mark of disrespect; he needed to move on to conclaves and conversations with diplomats and dignitaries. We were fortunate to have encountered him at all.

Only decades later did I hear anything more about the Coordinator of World Peace in Jerusalem. A Jerusalem weekly for local news reported that the staff of a closed institution for adults struggling with mental illness had thrown a party to celebrate the 70th birthday of the staff's favorite resident, identifying him by name. No mention was made of his high-echelon rank or his ambitious vision.

Jerusalem is a city of dreams.

For me as a child, Jerusalem might as well have been merely a legend. At synagogue, we prayed about Jerusalem. On Friday nights, we added to the usual daily prayer for peace and wellbeing overnight a request that God guard not just us and all of God's people but also, specifically, Jerusalem. At the dramatic moment on Shabbat and holiday mornings when the Torah scroll is taken from its front-and-center cabinet, the Holy Ark, for a portion to be chanted from it, one line the congregation sings asks God to "rebuild the walls of Jerusalem." At the end of the most intense and holy day of the year, Yom Kippur, with the entire community present, the high drama of chants and a long blast of the shofar are followed by a final joyous cry (or song): *Le-shana ha-ba'a biYrushalayim—* "Next year in Jerusalem!" And the same expression of our most fervent aspirations as Jews recurs half a year later, at the final moment of the family-centered Passover *seder*. As a youngster, then, I imbibed the Jewish people's striving to, as the Psalmist put it (with the help of the King James Version translators), "hold Jerusalem above our chiefest joy" (Ps. 137).

I did, of course, become aware that Jerusalem, and all the Land of Israel, is a very real place. Just three months after I celebrated becoming a *bar mitzvah*, Jewish communities around the world held their breath as Syria and Egypt built up forces at Israel's borders, blocked naval access from the south, and seemed bent on destroying the State of Israel and slaughtering or expelling its Jewish citizens. Israel's seemingly miraculous victory in the Six Day War led to the reunification of Jerusalem, and American Jews' homes over the following year resounded with the recorded performance of Naomi Shemer's recently composed "Jerusalem of Gold," which had been transformed from an elegy of longing into a paean of praise and a song of love for the city's "mountain air pure as wine" and its unique landscapes of "gold, copper, and light."

My favorite *bar mitzvah* present was a portable shortwave radio, on which I tuned in the international broadcasts of radio stations around the world. The most exciting moment in my pursuit of radio signals skipped off the upper atmosphere and down to my home in a Boston suburb was the afternoon when I heard an announcer begin a broadcast with: "This is the Voice of Israel, broadcasting from Jerusalem." At the end of the short (perhaps 15-minute-long) magazine of news, culture, and music came *Ha-tikvah*, the anthem of the Jewish people and the Jewish state, with which I was familiar: "...to be a free people in our own land, the land of Zion and Jerusalem." Suddenly *Ha-tikvah* became, in a new way for me, the real anthem of a real place and a real city, just as real as Prague and London and Moscow and Washington, to whose stations I tuned in frequently. I was moved to tears.

The aspirations evoked by every mention of Jerusalem begin with the Hebrew Bible, as I was reminded on my first evening in the city. From the outset, those dreamlike aspirations were never limited to "seeking the welfare of Jerusalem" or a tranquil and prosperous life for its inhabitants (as the Psalmist writes in Ps. 122), nor even the greater glory of the wider Jewish people alone. "For from Zion shall instruction go forth, and the word of the Eternal from Jerusalem," wrote Isaiah, describing what would happen when the nations of the world come to that city to seek God's instruction in how best to live, as individuals and as societies (Isa. 2). The same peculiar, even astounding blend of ethnocentricity and universalism is expressed in Deuteronomy 4:6, which portrays the other nations observing the people Israel living in its promised land according to Israel's unique laws and remarking, "Surely that great nation is a wise and discerning people"—and presumably adopting at least some Israelite laws as their own.

The Bible's view of Jerusalem's centrality in an eventual universal recognition of the one God and God's demanding moral code echoes throughout Jewish literature. It underlies the crescendo at the end of the semi-official Prayer for the State of Israel, composed in 1948 and recited by Jewish communities around the world: "Appear in Your glorious majesty over all the dwellers on the earth, and let all who breathe declare, 'The Eternal, God of Israel, is Sovereign, and His sovereignty has dominion over all.'"

Jerusalem's dreamers do not have to invent a tradition of Jerusalem's crucial and central role in universal redemption. The Jewish tradition supplies it ready-made.

II. The City That Brings All Jews Together

It is a truism equally accepted among scholars of Jewish studies in academic settings and among teachers of Torah (in its broad sense, meaning all the Jewish religious tradition) that anyone who tells you that this or that position is "the Jewish view" of whatever subject it may be is either misinformed or deliberately misrepresenting Jewish culture and civilization. There is no one Jewish view of anything—not of God, not of history, not of any but the broadest of points in Jewish law and practice. There is no central authority among Jews, not only among ideological camps but even among Jews of the same religious or ideological stripe. Jewish Orthodoxy is divided and subdivided, Masorti/Conservative rabbis hold conflicting opinions, Reform leaders have basic disagreements within their fold, Zionists cannot come together over how to prioritize the goals of their movement, and Jewish secularists are not in basic agreement about which aspects of Jewish culture should be preserved in a post-religious era.

All those groups, with all their sectarian diversity, have their adherents in Jerusalem. Jewish thinking and practice run amok in the Holy City, which is also the capital of the secular state created by Zionism. The result may be a splendid panoply, a crazy quilt of diversity—or a cacophony of conflicting tones, chords, and registers.

Jewish Jerusalem—speaking for the moment only of its predominantly (or entirely) Jewish neighborhoods and setting aside for a moment its Christians and Muslims, its Arabs and Armenians and every other ethnic minority—is not so much one bastion of Jewish culture as an archipelago of Jewish lifestyle choices. The differences often give a distinctive look and feel to different neighborhoods. There is jostling among Jews, with secular pitted against religious. Among the adherents of Orthodoxy, separatist Haredi Jews ("ultra-Orthodox," their opponents call them) are pitted against the "nationalist religious" Orthodox Jews. The former are suspicious of Zionism and all it has wrought, while for the latter the state and society that Zionism forged are the apotheosis of Jewish expression.

An American consular official once expressed to me how baffled he was by the different sorts of head coverings that set apart the pro-Zionist and non-Zionist religious communities, not to mention the subtle complexities of dress that identify the members of various Haredi communities, both Hasidic and anti-Hasidic. He suggested someone publish a "field guide to Jewish dress" in Jerusalem, like the "field guides" to birds and flowers. The book would enable the uninitiated to sort out the fabric colors in the suits the men wear, the types of head covering that women adopt for modesty, and the shape and design of the fur-trimmed *shtreimel* of each Hasidic rebbe's followers.

Jerusalem is a carnival of Jewish options. For me, as an adherent, and indeed a rabbi, of one of the smallest of the religious ideological "streams" in Israel, Masorti Judaism (or as it is known in North America, where it has a larger presence, Conservative Judaism), Jerusalem is unique in all of Israel. There is nowhere in Israel but my corner of Jerusalem where I can choose which of three Masorti synagogue communities I'd like to walk to on a Shabbat morning. In addition, there are several nominally Orthodox congregations where the practice of Judaism has adopted the gender-egalitarian norms pioneered decades earlier in my own movement, and Reform congregations whose liturgy and practice are not nearly as far afield from tradition as among Reform congregations where I grew up, in North America. In this city whose image is one of radical divisions between secular and fervently religious Jews—this city, of all places—I have a wider variety of synagogue options than almost anywhere else on earth. The school system too, in this city, enables groups of parents and educators to craft schools with a variety of approaches and ideologies regarding Judaism (and pedagogy), from Reform Judaism, open to the world's cultures, to Haredi schools that teach little or nothing of mathematics, English, or history, concentrating solely on sacred texts.

Like light refracted through a prism, Jewish civilization encountered modernity and fragmented into a rainbow of ideas, priorities, and ways of life. Living in Jerusalem is living in that full rainbow. And yet the Jewish segment of the city fulfills the promise of a midrash that interprets the phrase "a city bound together" (*'ir she-ḥubbera lah*) in Psalm 122 as "a city that makes all the people Israel comrades" (*ḥaberim*). Jerusalem's Jews do manage, in our diversity, to live together.

III. Tripping Over History

Near my present home in Jerusalem's Talpiyyot neighborhood—a Jewish suburb first settled in the 1920s and 1930s that was joined to the city only after 1948—are, along with remnants of Stone Age human settlements, indications of Jewish life in the Jerusalem area over many centuries. These include the excavated remains of a First Temple-period royal fortress. Nearby is a Jewish village from Second Temple times discovered accidentally by archaeologists exploring the Roman aqueduct system that brought water to Jerusalem from thirteen kilometers to the south. Jumping ahead to the modern era, a short walk away are the preserved historic homes of some of the outstanding figures in Jewish culture in the twentieth century: Eliezer Ben-Yehuda, credited with doing more than any other individual to revive Hebrew as a spoken language, and Shmuel Yosef Agnon, the only Hebrew author to have been awarded the Nobel Prize in Literature.

When I visit the Old City of Jerusalem, the timeline of Jewish history around me begins with the Kings of Israel and Judah, as it does near my home, but also includes points for medieval and early modern Jews. I think of the defenders of Jerusalem who fought alongside their Muslim neighbors against the invading Crusaders. There is the site of the synagogue established for Jerusalem's tiny Jewish community by Nahmanides, the great Catalonian rabbi who arrived in 1266. Here is the rebuilt Hurva Synagogue founded originally by Rabbi Yehuda He-Ḥasid, who brought hundreds of Jews from Central Europe to settle in Ottoman Jerusalem in 1700. On that site too in 1920, Sir Herbert Samuel, a newly arrived British Jew serving as the first High Commissioner of Mandate Palestine, chanted the passage from Isaiah 40 about the restoration of the Jews from exile: "Comfort, oh comfort my people, says your God. Speak tenderly to Jerusalem and declare to her that her term of service is over, that her iniquity is expiated.... Clear in the desert a road for the Lord!... Let the rugged ground become level and the ridges become a plain...." Hearing those words sung by the first Jewish governor of the Land of Israel in centuries, even one serving at the behest of a foreign empire, brought tears to the eyes of those assembled at the Hurva Synagogue that day.

In Jerusalem, you cannot help but trip over history.

Driving in Jerusalem one day in the 1990s, I stopped at a traffic light facing the big International Convention Center near the northwest edge of the city. The hourly news on the radio included this item: the Israel Antiquities Authority was suing the non-governmental Jewish Agency for Israel, which owns the convention center, for allegedly violating antiquities law. The archaeologists claimed that in the construction of a new parking facility—directly in front of my eyes at that moment—the builders had destroyed the archaeological record of an encampment of one of the Roman legions that had laid siege to rebellious Jewish Jerusalem over nineteen centuries earlier. Reminders that many centuries of history are underfoot are a daily occurrence in Jerusalem.

Having chosen decades ago to make my life in Jerusalem, I am constantly made aware of my place in the long sweep of Jewish history. History cannot determine our past, but it enables us to gain insight into what has made us who we are.

Jerusalem's history does not define me, but it shapes me every day. Jerusalem is home to me not because a tiny part of it belongs to me; Jerusalem is home because I am part of what belongs to Jerusalem.

IV. The Neighbors

My work as a rabbi often brings me to the Old City, to the archaeological park just inside the Dung Gate, where Jewish prayer groups can meet without separating worshippers by gender. Families come from around the country and around the world to celebrate their children's arrival at the age of *bar mitzvah* or, for girls, *bat mitzvah*. I help them make it happen.

In the neighborhood outside the Dung Gate, Silwan, as in most of the city, parking spots are hard to find. I long ago gave up driving to the Old City, preferring instead to travel by taxi. There are two routes from Talpiyyot to the Dung Gate. One passes through Jewish neighborhoods and into the Old City via the Jaffa Gate. The other, more direct, passes through the Arab neighborhoods Abu Tor and Silwan. Jewish taxi drivers are often reluctant to travel that route, for fear of encountering rock-throwing teenagers or other forms of violence. My assessment is that their fear is almost totally groundless. After all, I myself used to drive that route and park in Silwan, and only the scarcity of parking keeps me from doing so now. Trying to save time and money on those trips, I often order a taxi from a local dispatcher, almost all of whose drivers are Arab residents of Jerusalem.

In the autumn of 2016, a spate of stabbing attacks against Israeli Jews by young Palestinians had the city on edge. Whenever such a period of tension occurs, even the limited contact between Jews and Arabs in Jerusalem is curtailed. Both sides, for example, shy away from public parks that border both Jewish and Arab neighborhoods, where the two communities normally walk and picnic side-by-side, even if not actually together. In such periods, Jewish taxi drivers are even more adamant about avoiding Arab neighborhoods, so during those months I regularly sought out Arab taxi drivers to bring me to the Dung Gate any morning I needed to be there.

Something shifted unexpectedly (for me). The Arab drivers were happy to take me where I was going, but none of them would drive me through Abu Tor and Silwan to get there. They were afraid that with such a passenger, a pale Ashkenazi Jew with a skullcap on his head, they might have rocks thrown at their windshield. Better to take the longer, safer route.

What would anyone elsewhere in the world have thought would change in my routine during a period of Arab-Jewish tension in Jerusalem? Would they not assume that I would double down on my isolation from my Arabic-speaking neighbors? Who would have imagined that instead of me viewing the Arab taxi drivers as a potential problem, *I* would be perceived by *them* as a potential problem?

Jerusalem is two cities, or perhaps more like a cell in the midst of mitosis (or its opposite)—not quite one, but not quite two either.

Another metaphor for our shared but dual existence is the rhetorical pattern called "hendiadys," the expression of a single idea by two words connected with "and," such as "nice and warm" or "sick and tired." Each individual term means something, but together they mean something else, something different from the sum of two parts.

To be a Jew in Jerusalem—and, I imagine, to be part of the Arabic-speaking population of the city—means something different because of the presence of neighbors who are "other," who see the world differently, who live according to another calendar. It is not the only city in Israel with a mixed population, but it is the only one with its particular history of division and of forced reunification under Israeli rule nineteen years after the 1948-1949 war.

The house in which my family has lived for twenty years, in Talpiyyot, is built on land purchased by Jews in the 1920s for the establishment of the new suburb, but my wife and I own an apartment in nearby Bak'a. That neighborhood was a comfortable middle-class Arab and Armenian neighborhood until its inhabitants fled in the spring of 1948. After the war, the homes and vacant lots were considered "abandoned property," and in the 1950s the new State of Israel granted the homes to new immigrants, often dividing large dwellings into several housing units, and made the vacant lots available to developers for the construction of apartment buildings. The lot on which our apartment is located was one of those empty lots.

I have never researched the land registry records, but presumably a Palestinian Arab family, or an Armenian family, that was not within the armistice lines in 1949, owned that land and has never been compensated for what they lost. That too is part of living with history closing in on you from all sides in Jerusalem.

V. Welcome Home

Growing up in Boston, at least when I did, one was taught implicitly that New England, and specifically the "Hub of the Universe" (or just "the Hub," as Boston is called in local newspaper headlines), was the pinnacle of human civilization. As a child, I pictured living all my life in Massachusetts. But the call of Jerusalem was ever stronger, especially as my individual fate was unexpectedly caught up in the fate of Jerusalem (and indeed of all the country). My first visit, as I noted, came in mid-September 1973—three weeks before the Yom Kippur War brought a year of misery, suffering, and sacrifice to so many Israelis. It was difficult to leave after that. I stayed two years instead of one.

By 1976, when I was here on a visit, on a street in Jerusalem I happened to encounter a revered teacher of mine from my earlier two-year stay. "Peretz," he said, "welcome home!" At that moment, my consciousness of where home is for me shifted to match what had been in my heart already. About six weeks later back in Massachusetts, I met a lovely young woman who told me that when she was finished with her B.A., she would move back to Jerusalem. We have been there together for 35 of the last 40 years.

My adult children grew up in this kaleidoscopic city, where liberal democracy and fervent religiosity (of many sorts), ancient history and biotech innovation all mix, where the air resounds at various times with church bells, the voice of the *mu'ezzin*, and the Friday afternoon siren announcing Shabbat candle-lighting time. All three of my children benefited from the city's diversity, its high culture, its fine university. All three were within 100 meters of suicide bombers over a four-day period in 2002. (All were unscathed.) Instead of the wedding of an older friend, it was her funeral that my then-14-year-old daughter attended the day after the young woman was killed in a suicide bombing.

Life in Jerusalem is intense, sometimes heartbreaking, often exhilarating. I would not trade it for a life anywhere else, even in what a friend once called "the sylvan serenity of New England." Jerusalem has become my home.

5.

My Love of Jerusalem as a Reform Jew
Laurence P. Malinger

I was blessed to attend the Greene Family Camp in Bruceville, Texas, during my childhood years. One of the wonderful blessings of attending the Reform Movement's summer camp was the integration of staff from Israel and around the world. It was there, in the hill country of central Texas, as the sun set over the hills on Friday nights, when we welcomed the Sabbath, where I fell in love with the city of Jerusalem.

We were taught an amazing song, *Yerushalayim shel Zahav*—"Jerusalem of Gold," written by Naomi Shemer. The lyrics weave together biblical references as well as traditional Jewish poetry and themes, addressing exile and longing for Jerusalem. As I have learned, at the time the song was written, the Old City of Jerusalem was under Jordanian control. Jews had been banned from the Old City and the rest of Jerusalem east of it, losing their homes and possessions and becoming refugees. They were barred from either returning or entering the areas, and many holy sites were desecrated and damaged during that period.

The Israel Forever Foundation provides the following remarks on its website:

> On June 5th, only three weeks after the song was published, the Six-Day War began. When, on the third day of the war (June 7, 1967 / 28 Iyar 5727) IDF Paratroopers gained the Temple Mount, the song

"Jerusalem of Gold" burst from their lips. It was a natural expression of 2000 years of yearning for that moment, an expression of joy that the heart of Zion was finally returned to the Nation of Israel.

They were the physical embodiment of a miracle. Can you imagine that feeling? Although the State of Israel was officially re-established in 1948, it was the moment when Jewish sovereignty was regained in the holiest place on earth for the Nation of Israel that we were a people truly reborn.[34]

The lyrics of the song create an image of majestic mountains with pure air and a scent of the trees. We hear the church bells, all in the middle of a walled city. A city that is known as Jerusalem, filled with light shining forth to all. Just the very nature of one's sight of this city causes many songs to come forth.[35]

Singing and celebrating in this sacred place, my summer home for more than a decade, enabled me to envision my personal connection to the City of Jerusalem as we also had hills and clean air surrounding us. In the summer of 1988, when I began my studies to become a rabbi at the Hebrew Union College-Jewish Institute of Religion's Jerusalem campus, it was there that I began the process of exploring this vibrant city, interwoven with both ancient and modern connections. I walked the cobblestones of the Old City, through each of its quarters representing the faiths of many. In the Jewish quarter, I climbed down the steps outside of the Western Wall, the last outer remnant of the Second Temple. It was there, as I gazed

---

34. "Yerushalayim Shel Zahav—יְרוּשָׁלַיִם שֶׁל זָהָב," Israel Forever Foundation, https://israelforever.org/interact/multimedia/yerushalayim_shel_zahav/.

35. Ibid.

over the Old City of Jerusalem, that I appreciated the majesty of this sacred place.

The Hebrew Bible refers to Jerusalem by name some 700 times, and as Zion (which refers to the Temple Mount, and later came to designate Jerusalem as the capital city, and thus eventually the Holy Land as a whole) some 150 times. But these hundreds of explicit references to Jerusalem and Zion by name are, of course, only the tip of the Biblical iceberg; the implicit references cannot even be counted. Post-Biblical Jewish literature similarly reflects Jerusalem's central significance. Rabbinic literature, the Talmud and Midrash, is replete with explicit and implicit references to Jerusalem, as is the classical Jewish liturgy.

As a result of Jerusalem's being the national capital and the site of the Temple, the only place in which the Biblical sacrificial cult could thereafter be properly maintained, Jerusalem and the Temple attained a special status of sanctity in later Jewish law. With the destruction of Jerusalem and Solomon's Temple by the Babylonians in 586 BCE, the Jews in Babylonian exile now faced a new problem: how to survive and function religiously despite the loss of Jerusalem as both their national and religious center. The problem was expressed most eloquently by the psalmist in words which became, in subsequent centuries, a sort of Jewish pledge of allegiance:

> By the rivers of Babylon, we sat down and cried,
> as we remembered Zion.
> On the willows therein
> we hung up our harps.
> For there our captors asked us for songs,
> and our tormentors (asked us) for mirth:
> sing for us some of the songs of Zion.

But how can we sing the Lord's song
on foreign soil?
If I forget you Jerusalem,
let my right hand be paralyzed.
Let my tongue stick to the roof of my mouth,
if I do not remember you,
if I do not elevate Jerusalem
above my greatest joy (Psalm 137:1-6).

The significance is clear: the Jews had been removed from the heart of Zion, but Zion was never removed from the Jewish heart. The restoration of Jerusalem came to symbolize both Jewish national survival and fidelity to the Torah, and indeed eventually the hopes for the messianic era, when the Jews would be restored to Zion and Zion to the Jews. This is why the two most sacred ceremonies of the Jewish calendar, the fast day of *Yom Kippur* (the Day of Atonement) and the *seder* (the order of the service) on the evening of Passover, conclude with the words, *La'Shanah Ha-Ba'ah Bi-Yerushalayim* ("Next year in Jerusalem"). This also is why, to this day, the Jews, wherever in the world they may be, turn in prayer toward Jerusalem.

My studies introduced me to the understanding of the importance of our connection to the city of Jerusalem. I've learned that the meaning of the city's name is "Possession of Peace."[36] Others will translate it as a "City of Peace." Ideally, the symbolism of the City of Jerusalem is that of a place that enables many to live together in wholeness, or peace. This is what connects me strongly to this sacred city: the potential to be a place where everyone can get along, even with differing beliefs.

---

36. "Origin of Jerusalem," dictionary.com, https://www.dictionary.com/browse/jerusalem#:~:text=First%20recorded%20in%201580%E2%80%931600, peace%E2%80%9D%20(traditional%20interpretation).

I am a Reform Jew, and as a member of the Reform Movement, I agree with our commitment to accept and support the foundational aim of Zionism: the establishment of a Jewish state in Israel, the homeland of the Jewish people. This is simply a continuation of the early Zionist dream to foster a living, breathing national culture that represents the highest ideals of Jewish peoplehood. As we live in a world that still ostracizes the Jewish people, it is my desire for Jews to be free and liberated citizens of the world who also contribute as Jews to our global civilization.

The work of Zionism did not end when the State was established in 1948. We all strive to make the State of Israel a true inheritor of the prophetic tradition of the Jewish people: a nation devoted to pursuing justice and creating a complete world. My love for Israel is channeled into efforts that advance the vision of what I believe Israel can—and must—yet be.

I, as a proud member of the Reform Movement, believe that a Jewish state must be a democratic state that celebrates the pluralism of Jewish practice and identity. I celebrate the notion of *k'lal Yisrael*, the unity of the Jewish people. I seek to integrate Jewish tradition into the realities of the modern world, believing in individuals' right to shape their own Jewish identity and way of life. As such, I am part of an active, global network of Jews of all ages, united by our love for Israel and our commitment to securing an Israel that fulfills the promise of its founding document: "THE STATE OF ISRAEL will … foster the development of the country for the benefit of all its inhabitants; it will be based on freedom, justice and peace as envisaged by the prophets of Israel; it will ensure complete equality of social and political rights to all its inhabitants irrespective of religion, race or sex; it will guarantee freedom of religion, conscience, language, education, and culture…."[37]

---

37. "Declaration of Independence," Provisional Government of Israel, Tel Aviv, Official Gazette, No. 1 (5 Iyar 5708, May 14, 1948): 1, https://m.knesset.gov.il/en/about/pages/declaration.aspx.

Ever since my first visit in 1988, I have been back to Israel more than a dozen times. During each visit, I always make a stop in Jerusalem. It is there that I began my own journey toward my own Jewish identity as an adult. Nowadays, I am often troubled by the challenges of Jerusalem as a Reform Jew. Even though Jerusalem is considered the spiritual center of the Jewish people and has a deep and profound spiritual significance for many Jews, it is hard to feel that centrality and significance when there are members of the Jewish community, the Ultra-Orthodox, who reject my Jewish expression as valid and meaningful.

One of the sacred places in Jerusalem is the *Kotel*—the Western Wall, a remnant of the Temple Mount. It has become a synagogue in that it is a place to worship. At the *Kotel* itself, the plaza is separated into a men-only and a women-only section. I am respectful of the belief that some cannot pray in a mixed assembly. Further down, near Robinson's Arch, an egalitarian prayer section was built to allow the other streams of Judaism to pray together. I too can offer my sacred words in the holy city, along with my wife and daughter and friends, no matter their gender identity. Now, in the current state of the Israeli government, there is a newly elected leadership who want to deny my right to exist as a Reform Jew in the Jewish homeland. They want to remove my ability to join in prayer near the Temple Mount, a privilege denied to Jews only when the Old City was occupied by outside forces. My Jerusalem of Gold is becoming tarnished.

For many Jews, visiting Jerusalem is a deeply moving and spiritual experience, as it allows them to connect with their heritage and religious traditions in a profound way. The city is mentioned numerous times in the Hebrew Bible, and is the site of many important religious landmarks, including the Temple Mount and the Western Wall. It is often referred to as the "eternal capital" of the Jewish people and is considered a sacred space where Jews can connect with the divine. Anyone who disallows any Jew this opportunity is rejecting the possibility of the Jewish people coming together as one.

I will continue to visit Jerusalem and I will work side-by-side with allies to support a place that allows every Jew to be treated with respect and dignity and that is inclusive of all Jews. This is why the beginning of the words of Psalm 122 speak to me:

> I rejoiced with those who said to me,
>> "Let us go to the house of God."
> Our feet are standing
>> in your gates, Jerusalem.

Even though I have developed a romanticized relationship with Jerusalem, I also know my history and the reality of the world in the present day. As I teach, we must recall our history, personally, proudly, and unapologetically. First and foremost, we must do so because, in our over-indulgence in social media, where the retrieval of history is as fleeting as a Facebook feed, where Israel is labeled as Goliath and not David, our children and children's children must understand that the aggressions of the Middle East did not begin with Israel, but with a hostile Middle East that repeatedly denied the right of the Jewish state to exist and rejected the international accessibility of the City of Jerusalem to all three Abrahamic faiths.[38]

Second, and here let me tread carefully, we must know our history because we must know how very different the world is today from what it was years ago. Israel today is not the Israel of the 50s, 60s and 70s, and that is exactly the point. The question of Israel's policies toward the settlements and toward nurturing a two-state solution as well as its desire to

---

38. David Harris, "Why History Still Matters: The 1967 Six-Day War," Aish.com, https://aish.com/why-history-still-matters-the-1967-six-day-war/.

define what it means to be a Jewish state is a question whose answers lie in part but not entirely in Israel's hands. Like the biblical Samson, Israel must be cautious lest it cause the edifice to tumble down upon itself. To insist on framing our present moment as akin to the past is to do ourselves an intellectual and moral disservice in that it provides Israel a free pass on the manifold challenges presently on its docket. If we truly want our children and children's children to arrive years from now with the hoped-for outcome of an Israel at peace with her neighbors, then Israel and the pro-Israel community must stop viewing the world through the prism of 1967, 1948, and Masada.

Soon, I will travel again to Israel and ascend the mountain to enter the City of Jerusalem. When I walk on the cobblestones of the Old City, I wonder if any of my ancestors, exiled for thousands of years, could ever have imagined that their descendants one day would rejoice in *ir asher badad yoshevet, u-v'libah homah*, in the solitary city in whose heart lies a wall. And I smile inwardly with pride at the thought of what these ancestors would say if they knew that their descendants came to this sacred place in peace. I like to dream about the future, not stay in the past. I dream of a day when one of my grandchildren will stand in the Old City of Jerusalem, God willing, undisturbed in a Jewish state that lives at peace with her neighbors. It is a day of which I dream, a day for which we all pray. It is a day that we commit to working toward, doing all that is in our power to make happen. No different from preceding generations, as diaspora Jews we must always be ready to step up for Israel. That day, that golden sunrise signaling a new era, is not yet here. Like Jerusalem of Gold, its outline sits on the horizon just beyond our reach. And yet, in the darkness of the night its light still beckons. Distant as it is, it beckons us to draw near, as we ever so slowly approach to greet the dawn.

6.

Jerusalem, Our Common Mother City
Yehezkel Landau[39]

When I moved to Jerusalem from America in 1978, I chose to put my body where my Jewish prayers had already taken me. After watching the disturbing news emanating from the Holy City for years, I felt a strong need to be there, to experience the world from that unique vantage point and to contribute what I could to transforming the political conflicts that keep the city in the media crosshairs. As soon as I arrived, I felt at home. The pink stone facades just before sunset, the Muslim call to prayer reverberating from minarets, the sweet smell of jasmine, and the alluring fragrances of spices in the marketplaces, and, above all, the amazing diversity of people and cultures—all these features of that vibrant city nourished and elevated my spirit.

After living and working in Jerusalem for almost 25 years, I am again based in the northeast United States. Still, when I recite my daily prayers, my body is directed eastward toward

---

39. Portions of this reflection draw on a presentation given at the SIDIC Center in Rome in May 1995, which was later published under the title "Sharing Jerusalem: The Spiritual and Political Challenges" in the *SIDIC Journal,* Vol. XXIX, Nos. 2-3, 1996, pp. 3-9. The sponsors of that center and of my presentation were the Catholic community of Notre Dame de Sion, a community active for decades in promoting interfaith understanding. I refer to them later in this essay.

58

the Temple Mount.[40] Jewish mystical teachings view that sacred plateau as the holiest place in the cosmos. They speak of a Foundation Stone, *Even Hashtiyah* in Hebrew, which the Eternal One placed there at the time of Creation. In the Jewish worldview that I share, it is the epicenter of the universe; and it became the spot where the Holy of Holies stood in the two ancient Temples built there, the first by King Solomon and the second following the return from exile in Babylon. In my intuitive understanding, centuries of prayers directed toward that site have created a kind of Jewish force field, sustained until now by devout Jews the world over. We are like iron filings in a magnetic field, aligned with those spiritual vectors whenever we pray.

Even in exile, faithful Jews never forgot the holiness of Jerusalem, ceaselessly yearning to return to that Divinely consecrated place. Psalms 126 and 137, which feature prominently in our prescribed liturgy (especially before the Grace after Meals), are ancient and eloquent expressions of that centuries-long yearning. I share that longing, which was manifest in my nightly dreams and daily meditations even before I had the chance to leave North America and take up residence there. Still today, in many of my dreams I find myself in Jerusalem, walking its streets and enjoying its unique spiritual and cultural atmosphere.

In Psalm 87 there is another reverential description of Jerusalem, called "Zion" and "City of God." The psalmist seems to believe that each of us, "this one and that one," is born twice, receiving in a metaphorical sense two birth certificates. The first is for our bodies, which come into the world wherever

---

40. In the Jewish tradition, Jerusalem has been the only *qiblah*, the place for directing one's prayers, for millennia. I find it fascinating that Prophet Muhammad, peace and blessings be upon him, favored Jerusalem as the *qiblah* for the emerging *umma* (Muslim community) for about a year and a half, until he changed it to the *Kaaba* in *Makkah*/Mecca.

our mothers are at the time of our arrival. The second, a Divinely issued birth certificate, lists Zion/Jerusalem as our spiritual birthplace. I resonate strongly with this description of Jerusalem as our common Mother City, since I view it as the cosmic point of origin as well as of universal redemption.

As an interfaith educator and religious peacebuilder for over forty years, working to promote inclusive justice and genuine peace between Israeli Jews and Palestinian Arabs, these scriptural and kabbalistic teachings undergird the faith that has animated my efforts. I am dismayed and saddened by religious exclusivists who claim Jerusalem as the rightful domain of only one Divinely favored community—whether they be Crusader Christians in medieval times, their apocalyptic heirs of today, or militant Jews and Muslims who have supremacist ideologies sanctioning unholy wars that end up desecrating what they profess to be holy.

One of those exclusivists was, sadly, a former Chief Rabbi of Israel, the late Shlomo Goren.[41] He once cited the well-known Biblical passage (I Kings 3:16-28) in which his kingly namesake was asked to decide which of two harlots was the real mother of a contested infant. Since the false claimant was prepared to divide the child in two, while the real mother was ready to give up her baby to ensure its survival, the wise King Solomon understood whose claim was genuine. Engaging in

---

41. In this context, his name carries some irony. His first name is that of King Solomon, and his surname means "threshing floor," an allusion to the location that Solomon's father, King David, purchased from Aravna the Jebusite and which became the site of the first Temple. David, according to the Bible (I Chronicles 28:3), was disqualified from erecting that House of God because of the blood he had spilled during his years as a warring militia leader. It was left for his son, whose name derives from Shalom/Peace, to build the first Temple. The central altar in that Temple was made of uncut stones, ensuring that no implement that might have served as a weapon would be used in its construction. When I hear Jews and Christian Zionists calling for the erection of a third Temple in place of the Islamic shrines on the Temple Mount/Haram ash-Sharif, which could only happen through horrific warfare engulfing millions of people, I wonder what Bible these apocalyptic militants have read.

what we might call political *midrash*, Rabbi Goren argued that, since the Arabs want to divide Jerusalem into two capitals while the Israeli government wants it to remain united under its sole sovereignty, Israel is Jerusalem's true "mother" My own midrashic and political understanding is in total disagreement with this viewpoint. As I indicated in my reference to Psalm 87, this exclusivist notion reverses the Biblical metaphor by seeing the Holy City as a contested baby rather than the Mother City for various "children." As we know from our own experience, mothers (and fathers) can love their different children equally.

Rabbinic tradition is full of teachings that can, and should, be cited in the service of peacemaking rather than partisan politics. There is another *midrash*, in the compendium *Bereishit Rabba* (56:10), that offers an explanation for the origin of the Hebrew name for the Holy City, *Yerushalayim.* In Genesis 14, after Abraham rescues his nephew Lot, he comes to Jerusalem to be blessed by its king and distinguished priest, Melkhitzedek. The name of the city was then *Shalem*, suggesting wholeness or harmony. Melkhitzedek blesses Abraham (still called *Avram*) in the name of *El Elyon*, the Supreme God. Abraham was not the only monotheist at that time, and he accepted Melkhitzedek's bread, wine, blessing, and tithed offerings.[42] Two verses later, Abraham speaks to the king of Sodom, referring to the Divine in the same language: *El Elyon*, possessor of heaven and earth. So, Abraham and Melkhitzedek share a monotheistic vocabulary and use it to glorify God's name before others in Jerusalem. In the *midrash*, God immortalizes that encounter and that joint testimony by naming the city in honor of both the priest-king and the patriarch, with *Shalem* to acknowledge Melkhitzedek and placing in front of it *Yeru* to honor Abraham. Why *Yeru*? This

---

42. This is the first Biblical reference to the sacramental symbols of bread and wine, which later became central elements in Jewish and Christian rituals.

is a slight variation on (*Adonai*) *Yireh*, the name that Abraham himself gives to Moriah, the Temple Mount, at the end of the Binding of Isaac drama eight chapters later. The text in Genesis 22 explains this name as meaning that God will be revealed, or made manifest, there.

In this rabbinic source, which unfortunately few Jews are aware of, we are taught that *Yeru-Shalem* testifies to a pluralistic monotheism, as seen and sanctioned from God's vantage point. Moreover, the plural ending on *Yerushalayim* suggests that the multiplicity inherent in the city's holiness goes beyond two monotheisms to embrace the manifold community of communities encompassing all believers in the One Supreme God.[43]

These and similar Jewish teachings continue to inspire me. Wherever I happen to be located, Jerusalem is my spiritual home. However the mystics of different faith traditions imagine a celestial Jerusalem as a template for messianic transformation on the earthly plane, the terrestrial Holy City is an ambivalent place, a source of hope as well as tragic conflict. It has been for centuries a contested prize for religious warriors. Today, it is the heart of the conflict between Israelis and Palestinians. I use the "heart" metaphor deliberately, for I find it useful as a

---

43. I would add a parenthetical but important comment here. To the south of Jerusalem is the city where Abraham lived, *Hevron*/Hebron. Its Hebrew name derives from the same root as does *haver*, or "friend." The Arabic name for the city, *Al-Khalil*, also means "the friend" and is a reference to Abraham/Ibrahim, the beloved friend of God (see, for example, II Chronicles 20:7 and Isaiah 41:8). The patriarch bought the cave of *Makhpelah* there as a burial site for his wife Sarah when she died. He did not conquer it or even claim it before Ephron and his fellow Hittites, even though God had promised him five times before Genesis 23 that his descendants would inherit the entire land. *Makhpelah* in Hebrew means "multiplicity"—so encoded in the names of the two holiest places in the Holy Land, *Yerushalayim* and *Makhpelah*, is the idea of a multiple or pluralistic sanctity. Such a perception should call forth from all monotheistic believers an inclusive understanding of what our consecrating roles should be at and around these sacred places, if we wish to honor the legacy of Abraham, who is our common forefather just as Jerusalem is our common mother.

symbolic lens. I see the four quarters of Jerusalem's Old City
(Jewish, Christian, Muslim, and Armenian) as akin to the four
chambers of a human heart, pumping spiritual vitality through
two bodies politic, Israel and Palestine. But this holy heart is
also suffering from "cardiac" disease, coronary stenoses or
blockages that endanger the health and ultimate survival of
both political entities. The diplomats and politicians who will
eventually have to negotiate a final status peace agreement
will need to create a framework in which the two national
communities undergo amputations of their symbolic bodies.
This means that the State of Israel (*Medinat Yisrael*) will be
smaller than the Land of Israel (*Eretz Yisrael*) and the State
of Palestine (*Dawlat Filastin*) will be smaller than the Land
of Palestine (*Ard Filastin*). Courageous political and religious
leaders on both sides will need to help the two peoples grieve
the loss of their maximalist dreams and aspirations. At the
same time, the political surgeons will have to leave the shared
heart, *Yerushalayim/Al-Quds*, whole and intact, whatever the
mutually acceptable arrangement for joint sovereignty.[44]

Even before a peace agreement is negotiated, Jerusalem
is perhaps the world's premier laboratory for interreligious
encounter and cross-fertilization. The sad reality is that
political pollution prevents the city from realizing its potential
as a center for spiritual interaction and shared blessing. Still,
even with its current impediments, I have been privileged to
participate in many interfaith activities and programs involving
both local residents and visitors from many countries. As the
Israeli-Palestinian conflict moves toward resolution, many
more people will come as pilgrims, students, and long-term

44. Years ago, I saw an issue of *People* magazine with conjoined twins on the cover
who were joined at the heart. There was no way to separate them without killing at
least one of them. Israel and Palestine are in a similar situation, sharing a common
heart that must remain physically united and spiritually healthy.

residents, adding their religious and cultural perspectives to the mix.

I do not want to indulge in premature celebration, since I am pessimistic in the short run even as I remain hopeful for the future. (I have an infant granddaughter living outside Tel Aviv, and I have her and her generation in my heart and mind.) I know how painful and stressful the present situation is for those who live in the Holy City. I am cognizant of the power imbalance that favors Jewish interests and disadvantages those of Palestinians, many of whom cannot even live in the city because Israeli government policy prevents them from returning to their original homes there.

Although Israeli officials like to speak of Jerusalem as the "eternal and undivided capital of Israel," the reality on the ground is of two national communities (and other minorities, like the Armenians) under one political jurisdiction. Fear is a common denominator keeping the communities apart. I can share two illustrative experiences, each connected to my work as an interfaith educator, which brought this sad reality home. Both occurred during the first Intifada (1987-1993), when my son Raphael was a toddler. I was then living at the edge of West Jerusalem, not far from Hadassah Hospital in the neighborhood of Ein Kerem/Ein Karem.

In the first instance, I was scheduled to deliver an evening presentation at St. George's College, an Anglican institution in East Jerusalem where I often lectured. I was without my car that day and had to take a taxi, along with my son, across the city to give my presentation and lead a discussion. The Jewish taxi driver refused to take me there, saying he feared that his vehicle would be damaged by stone-throwing Palestinians. I tried to reassure him that the route was safe, but I was confronted by what the late political theorist Meron Benvenisti called "the geography of fear."[45] In the end, the driver agreed to let me off at the American Colony Hotel, and I walked with Raphael the short distance from the hotel to the college.

In the second illustration, I was on my way to give another lecture, this time at the Ecce Homo center on the Via Dolorosa, where the Catholic community of Notre Dame de Sion (NDS) ran a Biblical Studies program for priests and nuns from all over the world. My usual route to the Lions' Gate, where I parked my car and walked up the street to Ecce Homo, took me through the Palestinian neighborhood of Wadi el-Joz. Many Jewish Jerusalemites had their cars repaired by Palestinian mechanics in that neighborhood, and it was a part of the city where mutually beneficial commercial relations prevailed over politics. But on the day in question, municipal elections were being held, and that raised the level of political confrontation. As I drove up a hill in Wadi el-Joz, I saw a Likud Party campaign car, identifiable by its markings, on fire in front of me. Apparently, someone had thrown a Molotov cocktail at the car. I was shocked to see this flaming vehicle and horrified to see its driver rolling on the ground nearby, his clothes also on fire. Several Palestinians had gathered to help douse the flames and save the driver from serious injury. Instinctively, I put my car into reverse and sped away, reaching a nearby

---

45. Benvenisti served for a time as deputy mayor of Jerusalem. In his book *Conflicts and Contradictions* (New York: Villard Books, 1986, p. 196), he recounted an odd, but illustrative, incident concerning how the Holy City should be called in official Israeli communications: "In 1967, after the occupation of the Old City, the government insisted on the use of the name *Urshalim* in Arabic-language broadcasting. [N.B.: No Arab anywhere would adopt *Urshalim* in place of the traditional Arabic name for Jerusalem, *Al-Quds*, meaning 'The Holy']...At the time I was administrator of the Old City, I made a tacit agreement with the Israeli Broadcasting Authority that we use the traditional name, and one morning the radio began its broadcast in Arabic with the announcement: *Saut Israil min al-Quds* ('The Voice of Israel from al-Quds'). This caused a furor that reached the Cabinet. I insisted on knowing why they wanted to force the Arabs to call a city holy to them by a fabrication, a Hebrew name transmogrified into Arabic. The answer was that the use of *Urshalim* established a political fact: Jewish rule in Jerusalem. Eventually a compromise was reached. The name would be hyphenated and the city would be known officially in Arabic as *Urshalim-al Quds*. And so it has remained."

Border Police station and alerting those inside to what was happening. I then returned home and called the NDS sisters to let them know why I could not make it to that week's class. For the remainder of the course, I met the students at the Notre Dame Catholic center outside the New Gate, a venue that seemed safer amid the sporadic violence characteristic of that time period. Since I had recently become a father, my parental responsibilities took precedence over my work, and I had to make some prudent compromises that took the tragic reality around me into account.

Psalm 122 remains one of my favorite poetic passages from the Hebrew Bible:

A Song of Ascents, of David:
I rejoiced when they said to me,
Let us go to the House of the Eternal;
when our feet stood within your gates, O Jerusalem!
Jerusalem, built as a city
whose parts are linked together;
There the tribes used to go up,
the tribes of the Eternal –
as was enjoined upon Israel –
to give thanks to the name of the Eternal.
For there the thrones of judgment stood,
thrones of the house of David.
Pray for the peace of Jerusalem:
May they who love you prosper.
May there be peace within your ramparts,
and tranquility within your palaces.
For the sake of my brethren and friends,
I will say,
Peace be within you;
For the sake of the House of the Eternal our God,
I will seek your good.

As I pray with the psalmist for the peace of Jerusalem and all its inhabitants, I consider myself a faithful realist, aware of the social and political obstacles to genuine peace in and around the Holy City. The psalmist acknowledges that this holy city brings together two kinds of authority: the political or temporal, along with the religious or spiritual. This was the case already in the time of Abraham and Melkhitzedek when the latter was both the king and the high priest of the city. Combining these two disparate dimensions is a mixed blessing, since politics is the realm of the possible, usually requiring negotiated compromises, while religion is too often the realm of the absolute, making compromises elusive, if not impossible. Balancing these two aspects of human life in a place held sacred by several religious traditions is an almost super-human challenge, especially since both Judaism and Islam do not, in principle, acknowledge a desacralized social or political realm. History is full of instances when armies fought to establish unilateral control over the sanctuaries and palaces in Jerusalem, where the psalmist envisioned peace and tranquility prevailing. In our time, we are faced with the same extraordinary challenge: how to ensure that Jerusalem lives up to its vocation as the City of Peace. To realize this sublime vision, different religious communities must work together as partners in consecration while, at the same time, two national communities create a framework for sharing political sovereignty.

If we return to the metaphor of Jerusalem as a diseased but holy heart, a healing path to inclusive justice and genuine peace may lead through the pluralistic geography of her four quarters.

The ecumenical Christian Quarter resounds with the diversity of Christian life present in Jerusalem for two millennia. I will leave it to Christians to decide whether this diversity is a positive sign of "multiplicity" within the Christian family, or whether the separate chapels within the Church of the Holy Sepulchre signify a lamentable fragmentation among the different Christian communities.

One Christian community has a separate quarter unto itself: the Armenians. They were the first people to adopt Christianity *en masse* as their national faith, in the year 301. The Armenians are a deeply devout people, and their small Jerusalem community (numbering some 1,500 people) is centered around the ornate Cathedral of St. James. When one considers the distinctness of Armenian Christians, the unique features of their history and faith, and then juxtaposes them to the Israeli Jews and Palestinian Muslims in adjacent quarters, a remarkable pattern reveals itself.

These three peoples—the Armenians, the Jews, and the Palestinians—are rooted in the Holy Land for centuries with their respective identities and traditions. One common aspect of their religious heritages is a three-fold loyalty: to a people, to a faith tradition, and to a particular land. (For the Jews and Palestinians, it is the same common homeland; for the Armenians, it is the land of Armenia in the Caucasus region.) Perhaps because of this shared basis for self-identification, the three peoples have undergone similar experiences, particularly in the twentieth century.

On the level of the physical body, all three peoples have endured traumas: first the Armenian Genocide before and during World War I; then we Jews passed through the valley of death during World War II; and since then, the Palestinians have suffered dispossession, disempowerment, and injury or death at the hands of virtually every other Middle Eastern people they have encountered. All three peoples have a subjective sense of being survivor communities, mourning their martyrs and proudly affirming their communal dignity.

On the level of the spirit, the three peoples share another common denominator. All have suffered exile from their respective homelands during the last century. We Jews, of course, know what it means to be refugees, "strangers in strange lands," for more than twenty centuries. Our yearning and expectation to return to Jerusalem helped sustain our faith, even under harsh and desperate conditions. If, in our time, we Jews have been blessed to return to the Holy City as a free, self-governing people, while the Armenians have their own country once again and the Palestinians are still struggling to achieve independence and sovereignty, what lesson could there be in this fateful intermingling of joy and sorrow?

One allegorical scenario in my imagination conveys the experience shared by these three "suffering servant" peoples, to use the Biblical language from Isaiah 52-53. It is of three traumatized individuals walking through darkness while holding candles, lit by their ancestors, to illuminate their way. All three wanderers long for their lost homelands. Each one fears that, out of the darkness, some enemy will launch an attack, adding to the cross-generational chain of victimhood. None of the three is able to trust others to help overcome the trauma or the dread of future atrocities.

Then, suddenly, the three wanderers converge—in Jerusalem—and their candles illumine each other's faces. Each experiences the shock of mutual recognition. And in the human faces is a reflection of something mysteriously divine, so that each can echo the wondrous exclamation of the wounded Jacob, renamed Israel, in Genesis 33:10: "For I have truly seen your face as though seeing the face of God."

Could such an awareness of common vulnerability, especially in an age when humanity as a whole is an endangered species, together with an appreciation of the sacred Image of God that we all bear, be essential elements of Jerusalem's transcendent nature as a messianic epicenter? Could this challenge of reconciling fearful, embittered hearts summon Jews, Christians, Muslims, and others to work together as partners in consecration so that our traumatic histories can be healed and we, in turn, can be truly liberated?

Israeli journalist Hirsch Goodman wrote in *The Jerusalem Report*, the magazine he founded and edited, these inspiring lines: "I would suggest that ... we all agree that Jerusalem become the symbol of reconciliation, the place where all peace talks are held ... Jerusalem should not become an 'international city,' but the shared and united capital of two peoples striving to live together. It should be a city with no internal borders, but a city whose parts are permitted to retain their geographic and ethnic uniqueness as a microcosm of Israeli-Palestinian coexistence."[46] I would extend this idea and affirm that the Holy City has the potential for becoming a microcosm of global coexistence on this planet, balancing the particularistic and the universalistic dimensions of the human condition. Human survival may well depend on achieving such a balance in an organic and viable way.

Up to now, the conflicts over Jerusalem have, all too often, evoked the worst traits in those who claimed to love her, including both Jews and Arabs today. But our holy Mother City has the capacity to evoke the best in us as well. Our common forefather Abraham/Ibrahim was promised, in Genesis 12:3, that "through you all the families of the earth shall be blessed." In order for Jews, Palestinians, Armenians, and others to share in this promised blessing, they will have to sacrifice their partisan, exclusive attachments to Jerusalem. Such mutual sacrifice in the service of inclusive justice and peace will not only help protect our bodies and liberate our spirits, but it will also spread healing and hope to the far corners of the earth— *insha'Allah, b'ezrat Hashem*, with God's help.

---

46. *The Jerusalem Report*, November 4, 1993, p. 56.

7.

On the Heavenly Jerusalem and the Earthly Jerusalem
Ron Kronish

Some Personal History

I have lived in Jerusalem for 43 years, much more than half of my life by now. I made *aliyah* (went up to live in the land of Israel) in June 1979, just a few weeks after finishing my studies for a doctorate in education at the Harvard Graduate School of Education. I came with my family straight to Jerusalem, the capital of the state of Israel and the spiritual capital of the Jewish people.

Since I spent a year of studies in Jerusalem in 1970-71 with my wife at the Hebrew University—during which time we became deeply attached to the land, the culture, and the people of Israel—we had decided that Israel would be our home and that we would live in Jerusalem. For a brief time, we contemplated living on a kibbutz in the northern part of Israel, but not for long. Jerusalem would be our home—the place where we would raise our children and the place that commanded our presence as Jews who wanted to live out our Jewish identity to the fullest in a state which we could call our own, where we felt we belonged, where we could make our own unique contributions to this emerging, exciting, and challenging society called Israel.

After we came to Israel, I held two jobs during my first two years. First, I was a post-doctoral research fellow at the Melton Center for Jewish Education of the Hebrew University on Mount Scopus in Jerusalem. Second, I was a senior educator and supervisor of the Institutes of Jewish Zionist Education, an agency that conducted informal educational seminars for Jewish high school youth throughout Israel on issues of Jewish and Zionist Identity. We asked the students to think deeply and carefully about what it meant to live as a Jew in a Jewish state, how they would express their identity, how they would relate to the non-Jews in our midst, and many more existential questions. I did this second job for seven years, based in Jerusalem but also traveling all over Israel. It was a great help to me in getting to know the country and all the essential issues that we faced at that time (all of which we continue to confront).

After spending a year and a half in the United States in 1986 and 1987, I came back to Jerusalem to serve as the director of an American Jewish organization for four years. It was during this time that I became acquainted with the field of interreligious dialogue in Jerusalem and in Israel. In 1991, together with a few other people, I founded a new organization called the Interreligious Coordinating Council in Israel (ICCI) which I directed for 24 years, until the end of 2014, when I retired. During this time, I engaged intensively with Jews, Christians, and Muslims throughout the city. I also planned and implemented dialogue and action projects with diverse groups of Palestinian Arabs and Israeli Jews for many years. In so doing, I discovered both the ideal and the real Jerusalem.

Heavenly Jerusalem and Earthly Jerusalem

According to Rabbi Art Vernon,[47] the concept of an ideal or heavenly Jerusalem appears to emerge in Jewish tradition in the second century CE. There is a midrash, a rabbinic homily, in the name of Rabbi Yochanan, a leading rabbinic figure in Tiberias in the early third century, who asserts, in part, that

47. Rabbi Art Vernon, "The Heavenly Jerusalem," in *My Jewish Learning*, https://www.myjewishlearning.com/article/the-heavenly-jerusalem/.

in the future the earthly and the heavenly Jerusalem will be reunited as one. This teaching is based on an exposition of Psalm 122:3, *Jerusalem built up, a city knit together.* According to the midrash, "knit together" means the uniting of the earthly Jerusalem with the heavenly Jerusalem as one. According to Rabbi Vernon:

> The midrashic literature from the second century on is filled with descriptions of the rebuilt Jerusalem of the future. Various Midrash texts describe its dimensions, the materials of which it will be built, and the regard in which it will be held in terms that can only be categorized as fantastic.

The rabbinic imagination contemplates the restored and rebuilt Jerusalem of the future. It imagines a heavenly Jerusalem. But is that the whole story? According to Rabbi Vernon, there is more to the story:

> The midrash in which Rabbi Yochanan is cited raises the question as to whether the heavenly Jerusalem is simply a template or mirror image of the earthly Jerusalem or a reality unto itself that one day will materialize on earth. From the context, it can be assumed that one rabbi believed that the heavenly Jerusalem exists intact regardless of the state of the earthly Jerusalem. Rabbi Yochanan seems to argue that it is only when the earthly Jerusalem is restored fully that the heavenly Jerusalem will be realized fully as well.

The Heavenly Jerusalem is the aspirational one—the pluralistic, open, inclusive, harmonious one—in which Jews, Christians, and Muslims could live together in harmony and peace. In this Jerusalem, we would all even be able to pray together in the "Holy Basin," the Old City of Jerusalem, and even on Temple Mount, where, according to the Prophet Isaiah,

My house shall be called a house of prayer for all peoples (Isaiah 56:7). According to this ideal, Jerusalem would be a city that is shared by Jews, Christians, and Muslims in a spirit of mutual understanding and continual cooperation. This, of course, is a messianic understanding of Jerusalem, one that we should aspire to and endeavor to make happen, at the same time as we realize that it may take a very long time to achieve it.

Part of this vision of Jerusalem is the idea that Jerusalem is meant to be a holy city (*ir hakadosh*), perhaps the holiest city in the world, according to some Jewish visions of this place. For example, in the traditional Jewish prayer of thanksgiving after eating a meal, we pray: *Let Jerusalem, the holy city, be renewed in our time. We praise You, God, for you rebuild Jerusalem with compassion.*

Indeed, the hope for the rebuilding of Jerusalem is part of the foundational nature of traditional Judaism. Another prominent example of this can be found at the end of the Passover seder, when we say: *Next Year in Jerusalem* (*L'shanah Haba b'yerushalayim*), which was once meant to be a messianic wish but has now become a reality! (Interestingly, in Israel, we say: *Next Year in a Rebuilt Jerusalem*, which implies that Jerusalem is already in the process of being rebuilt!) The central idea being expressed here is that Jerusalem should be holy, special, unique, different from all secular cities. This, of course, puts a heavy burden on Jerusalem, one that is very difficult to achieve now, but nevertheless one that we should continue to guide to consciousness, one to which we should persist in aspiring.

However, there is Earthly Jerusalem, the physical (as opposed to the metaphysical) Jerusalem, the real city with real people of flesh and blood, who struggle to live together in some form of complicated coexistence on a daily basis, despite the constant political, security, theological, and social challenges. Contemporary Jerusalem represents a very complex, sometimes convoluted reality, in which many factors make the idea of a heavenly Jerusalem just a distant dream or perhaps a wishful hope.

Today's Jerusalem is a city of contrasts, contradictions, and complications. Its demography is diverse, divided mainly between Palestinians and Jews. As of 2022, the Jews represent about 61 percent of Jerusalem, with the Palestinians at about 39 percent. Among the Palestinians, the overwhelming majority are Muslims and a small percent are Christians (whose presence is dwindling all the time). Among the Jews, there are major divisions, including the Ultra-Orthodox, Modern Orthodox, traditional Jews, and secular ones.

The biggest problem among the Jews is with the Ultra-Orthodox, most of whom reject modernity, pluralism, and tolerance, and have caused great tension via verbal and physical violence against Muslims and Christians (and Reform and Conservative Jews!) in recent years. Another serious problem emanates from the extremist so-called "religious Zionists" who establish purposely provocative "settlements" in many places in East Jerusalem, and work through various dubious organizations to displace innocent Palestinians, which also raises the level of tension often.

Among the Palestinians, there are similar problems with ultra-religious extremist Muslims and ultra-nationalist Palestinians who frequently seek to ignite the city via incitement to violence or actual violence, specifically acts of terror, which paradoxically make the lives of the Palestinians much worse. Some of this violence is initiated by people associated with Hamas, the fundamentalist version of Islam that dominates in Gaza and has people in East Jerusalem and the West Bank, or other Islamic groups, like the Islamic Jihad, whose sole agenda is "resisting Israel." Other times, the violence comes from individual Palestinians who are simply fed up with the humiliation of the ongoing Occupation or are taking revenge for home demolitions or killings or the jailing of relatives and friends. The harshness of the military occupation often drives some Palestinians to commit irrational acts of violence, since they feel that they have been driven crazy by so much oppression over so many years.

On the Palestinian side, there is also a special problem with Palestinian Christians in Jerusalem, whose presence has been dwindling for decades. This is a serious problem, which in recent years is causing local Christians much consternation and has received international attention, including protests from the Archbishop of Canterbury and others. Writing in the *Sunday Times* of December 19, 2021, the Archbishop of Canterbury and the Anglican Archbishop in Jerusalem warned of a concerted attempt by fringe, radical Jewish groups to drive Christians away from the Holy Land—which takes place against the "historic tragedy" of the Christian population's century-long decline.

> Last week, leaders of churches in Jerusalem raised an unprecedented and urgent alarm call. In a joint statement, they said Christians throughout the Holy Land have become the target of frequent and sustained attacks by fringe radical groups. In a joint statement they described 'countless incidents' of physical and verbal assaults against priests and other clergy, and attacks on Christian churches. They spoke of holy sites regularly vandalized and desecrated, and ongoing intimidation of local Christians as they go about their worship and daily lives.
>
> These tactics are being used by such radical groups 'in a systematic attempt to drive the Christian community out of Jerusalem and other parts of the Holy Land,' the Jerusalem church leaders said in their statement. It is for this reason that when you speak with Palestinian

Christians in Jerusalem today you will often hear this cry: 'In fifteen years' time, there'll be none of us left!'

Clearly there is growing concern that there are systematic attempts to force Christians out of Jerusalem by Jewish extremist groups like *Ateret Cohanim* and radical anti-Christian groups such as *Lehava* and settler groups that are often supported by radical right members of Knesset in Israel, such as Itamar Ben Gvir.

In addition, they are frequently taunted by some extreme Ultra-Orthodox Jews when they walk around the Old City of Jerusalem, and some of their churches have been vandalized in recent years by fanatic groups under the slogan of *Tag Mechir* (Price Tag). I have witnessed this myself via my involvement over more than a decade with a group called *Tag Meir* (Light Tag), which combats hate crimes via solidarity visits to institutions that have been damaged and people who have been injured and their families. Fortunately, this coalition of more than 50 Jewish groups in Israel represents the sane, humanistic, religious culture of Judaism, and gives some hope to local Palestinian Christians, who are living in fear of the radicals and who feel that they are trying to encourage them to leave the city.

The Political Context

Whether you view Jerusalem as heavenly or earthly or both, contemporary Jerusalem is part and parcel of a problematic political context.

Jerusalem today is the capital of the State of Israel. However, following the 1948 War of Independence, from 1948 to 1967, it was a divided city. Half of the city, which was on the eastern side, was part of the Hashemite Kingdom of Jordan. The other half was in Israel. After the Six-Day War of June 1967, the eastern side of the city was officially annexed to Western

Jerusalem, so that there is now officially (according to the government of Israel) only one Jerusalem, which is allegedly "united." However, most of the international community has never formally recognized this annexation, so it remains an ongoing issue in diplomacy. In the meantime, the reality on the ground is that Jerusalem remains a very divided city, even if there is no longer a border in the middle of it, as was the case between 1948 and 1967.

In the Oslo Peace Accords of 1993, it was agreed that the final status of Jerusalem would be negotiated by the parties to the conflict after five years of the interim agreement. But, unfortunately, this never happened, so that the official status of Jerusalem is still an issue in international diplomacy. This continues to cause anxiety, especially for the Palestinians in the city, who have been hoping for a long time that somehow Jerusalem would be shared, i.e., that there would be a capital for the State of Palestine in East Jerusalem and a capital for Israel in West Jerusalem. This dream has become very remote in recent years, as the peace process between Israel and the Palestinian Authority has become frozen.

Accordingly, Palestinians in Jerusalem, who make up almost 39 percent of the population of the city, remain in limbo. They are residents of Jerusalem and can vote in Jerusalem's municipal elections, but they cannot vote in either Israeli or Palestinian national elections. Moreover, even though they pay taxes in Jerusalem, they do not get their fair share of infrastructure so that building homes and apartments is very difficult for them. They often feel oppressed and humiliated, and live mostly in poverty, and endure the constant threat of house demolitions, since they often build illegally when there is no other way. Also, psychologically they feel that they are part of the Palestinian community in the West Bank (as opposed to being part of the community of Palestinian Arab citizens of Israel).

There are some prominent NGOs that try to address these issues, such as *Bimkom* and *Ir Amim*. But, until the governments of Israel and the Palestinian Authority enter serious and sustained negotiations to resolve the basic political problems in Jerusalem, these issues will continue to fester and disrupt the daily coexistence of Palestinian Arabs and Israeli Jews for a long time to come.

A Vision for Jerusalem Is Necessary

While the reality of Jerusalem can be harsh sometimes—with violent incidents that upset the delicate fabric of constrained coexistence that does in fact prevail daily, most of the time—there is still a need to return to keeping a vision of the ideal Jerusalem alive, of a city that we would like to inhabit, for the mutual benefit of Palestinian Arabs (Muslims and Christians) and Israeli Jews alike. Jerusalem must become an inclusive and tolerant city supporting all its citizens' rights, affording them all opportunities to lead meaningful and safe lives.

I asked a rabbi, a bishop, and a Muslim professor—all of whom have been active in peacebuilding efforts in Jerusalem with me for a long time—to share their visions of Jerusalem with the readers of this article.

Rabbi Tamar Elad-Applebaum, who is one of the leading young Masorti (Conservative) rabbis in Israel today (and is my rabbi at Kehillat Zion in Jerusalem), offered her thoughts:

> I would like to see Jerusalem become a holy city, in which there will be a shared life for all citizens. There should be a way for people to express their national feelings of belonging as well as their religious faiths. I would like to see a set of relationships in Jerusalem where everyone respects the other in a good and positive way. I would like to see Jerusalem as a 'place of prayer for all peoples' [*Isaiah* 56:7]. I would really love to see

Jerusalem as a city which provides the opportunity for all human beings to dream about their lives. Our lives should be filled with holiness and human dignity. There should be a place for everyone. It should be a city of *hesed,* where lovingkindness and justice are found among all the people, as our classical biblical prophets described it. I feel certain that this is possible.

One of the leading Christian peacebuilders in Jerusalem, Bishop Emeritus Munib Younan, is apparently very much in agreement with Rabbi Elad-Applebaum. He has devoted much of his life to thinking about how Jerusalem could become a city of peaceful coexistence. As an interreligious peace activist, and as a Lutheran world leader, he has always struggled for peaceful and just solutions to the question of how Jerusalem can somehow be shared among Jews, Christians, and Muslims, and he has developed his own ideas for this. Bishop Younan believes that Jerusalem has a special mission in the world. In both the present and the future, Jerusalem should be a unique city due to its holiness and spiritual history.

> As a religious leader, I feel that Jerusalem must be a city of peace, coexistence and tolerance, where the three faiths share in this city. I would like to see that the holy places are places of worship and prayer, not centers of conflict. Jewish, Christian, and Muslim places should be fully respected. That is a key for peace. Once you respect the other's holy place, there will be less conflict between the people of the different religions and nationalities in Jerusalem. I think that this idea is not messianic, but actually possible.

Professor Mohammed Dajani, the founder and chairperson of *Wasatia*, the Middle Way in Islam, who comes from a distinguished Palestinian family with deep roots in Jerusalem, also believes that Jerusalem must be shared by Jews, Christians, and Muslims.

> The city of Jerusalem has a special place in the consciousness of the great monotheistic Abrahamic religions. For thousands of years, the holy city of Jerusalem has been the vital center of worship for Judaism, Christianity, and Islam. To seek a solution to the issue, we need to filter out the religious zeal and the political rhetoric from the reality on the ground. A viable solution could be reached by recognizing the attachment of each faith to the city. Rather than working to exclude each other from entering it, join hands to make it a model city open to pilgrims from all religions.
>
> A win-win solution may be successfully achieved if Jerusalem is viewed in terms of the historic Old City embraced by the wall and excluding the modern new city that was created in the last century outside the wall. I believe the city should be reclaimed by both sides as a religious rather than a political capital.

All three religious leaders and interreligious activists share a vision for Jerusalem, which has guided them and still guides them in their peace activism.

Conclusion

I live in the Earthly Jerusalem, but I am inspired by the Heavenly Jerusalem, the one of my dreams and visions, the one imagined by Jewish Tradition. The Heavenly Jerusalem of pluralism, inclusiveness, holiness, justice, and peaceful coexistence is the one that inspires me, gives me hope, allows me to look forward toward a better future. In this ideal Jerusalem, followers of the main religions in the city—Judaism, Islam, and Christianity—will engage in dialogue and cooperate on projects of mutual interest. There will be no more need for terror and counter-terror operations. Respect for diversity and different opinions and lifestyles will reign. Religious, political, cultural, educational, and scientific leaders will work together for the betterment of all the citizens of the city.

But, in the meantime, down here on earth, in the real Jerusalem, we still have a lot of work to do to bring the real closer to the ideal in this very special city, which is holy to three major religions, and to which two nationalities are affiliated, the Palestinian people and the Jewish people. Yet, I submit that this is our imperative in the years ahead—to close the gaps, to bridge the differences, to make this a city that will inspire the whole world, a city of peace and harmony, in the spirit of the Prophet Isaiah (2:3): "For out of Zion will go the Teaching, and the Word of the Lord from Jerusalem."

8.

And All the Nations Shall Flow Unto It
Jonathan Golden

"And it shall come to pass in the last days, that the mountain of the Lord's house shall be established in the top of the mountains, and shall be exalted above the hills; and all nations shall flow unto it." (Isaiah 2:2)

"וְהָיָה בְּאַחֲרִית הַיָּמִים נָכוֹן יִהְיֶה הַר בֵּית־יהוה בְּרֹאשׁ הֶהָרִים וְנִשָּׂא מִגְּבָעוֹת וְנָהֲרוּ אֵלָיו כָּל־הַגּוֹיִם:"[48]

Invited to write about what Jerusalem means to me as a Jew, one conversation immediately comes to mind. A young Orthodox Jewish woman, a self-described settler from the West Bank, had come to participate in our Institute on Religion and Conflict Transformation at Drew University, a three-week seminar designed to impart leadership tools and skills to young emerging inter-religious leaders from around the world. I understood a remark she had made to mean that she viewed a Jew, me in this case, as less Jewish because I reside outside of the Holy Land. Though quite reassured in my own Jewishness, I did take slight exception to the general assertion that a Jew's commitment to the faith was somehow contingent upon where they lived. My soon-to-be friend would later clarify her comment to mean: "if one is Jewish, you must have Jerusalem in your heart." This sounded a lot more reasonable

---

48. Alexander Harkavy, translation, *The Twenty-Four Books of the Old Testament*, Vol. 2 (New York: Hebrew Publishing Co., 1916).

to me. And as a Jew, there is no doubt that Jerusalem holds a place in my heart.

Jerusalem is the city outside of the United States that I have visited the most (with Dublin and Sao Paulo as close seconds). At one point I lived there for just under a year. Some of the most formative and transformative moments of my life occurred in the Holy City. In fact, I attribute much of who I am today and the work I do to experiences I had and things I learned in Jerusalem.

My First Visit: Jerusalem through a Child's Eyes

It was the summer of 1978 when my parents, my brother, and I took our only family trip to Israel. My brother had become a Bar Mitzvah in December, just six months earlier, and like many Jewish American families at the time, we planned a family trip to coincide with my brother's Bar Mitzvah. He would be called again to the Torah, as Bar Mitzvah, at the Western Wall. We took a two-week group tour with a guide who had a thick mustache in the style of the renowned Israeli archaeologist Yigal Yadin. Walking through ancient ruins across the country—"we have here a collapsation," he would say—fired my imagination, no doubt contributing to my dream of becoming an archaeologist.

Though not yet ten years old at the time, I have many memories of that trip and of Jerusalem in particular. We would visit the Western Wall multiple times during the tour. I recall observing the first time I visited how quiet it was. There were people there, but the decorum was noticeable. I recall a feeling of expansiveness. It conjured an image for me somehow of a giant piazza in Rome during siesta—the vast stone plaza with many fewer people than expected. I had never been to Rome, nor to a real piazza for that matter, at that point in my life. I had, however, been to cathedrals in the U.S., and it felt more like that than any American synagogue I had ever been in.

After navigating the Old City's narrow, sinewy maze of alleys, there was a feeling of awe, to suddenly find oneself in a giant open space. Strangely enough, it was like the sensation I'd get at the old Yankee Stadium, where one would emerge from a cinder block cavern to a spectacular view of the expansive green outfield. It's a feeling like that of one who has discovered a wondrous place. It's a feeling I still get every time I visit. It wouldn't be until many years later that I would understand just how many people's lives had been disrupted, displaced in the heart of Jerusalem's Old City, in order to create that space.

Another stop in our tour of Jerusalem was the "Arab Market." I have a memory of an open-air market, but I don't quite recall if it was the *souq* in the Old City. The first time we went we had to leave the market sooner than planned. Because a suspicious package had been discovered in a garbage can, we were being evacuated. Real or not, it felt quite real for many of us on the tour. We'd been taught our entire lives that "*they* want to kill us." I really didn't know who "they" were. I'd been taught that surrounding Israel were hostile Arab states. But no one had ever really told me anything about Arabs, other than that they were enemies of Jews and Israel. Worse, the only ideas I had about Arab identity were racist caricatures on Looney Tunes and the other media on which I was raised. Ironically, those caricatures of Arab people bear many of the same tropes often used to depict Jewish people in an unfavorable light: large noses, hunched over, scheming, and plotting. Imagine if I, and all Jewish children, had been taught to humanize Arab and Muslim people, even if they were adversaries in a conflict. Could things be different? What if Arab and Palestinian children had been taught that Jews were people just like them? In truth, many people were both: an estimated 800,000 Jews went to Israel from Arab countries of the Middle East and North Africa, their language, culture, and cuisine extremely similar to those of Arabs. But once the identity lines had been drawn, it seemed there was no turning back.

The most impressionable moment for me on that trip involved a photo of a young boy with a goat. It was back at the open-air "Arab Market," I cannot recall exactly where. We had shopped around what seemed to be endless adjacent shops with souvenirs. As we gathered near the bus to depart, a young Palestinian boy, probably just a little older than I, with a small goat motioned toward me. Invoking the universally recognized clicking motion, he invited me to take his photo with the animal.

Using a small plastic Kodak Instamatic—a cheap, popular camera at the time—I snapped a photo, smiled, and said thank you. The boy immediately put his hands together in a gesture that I knew meant he was asking for money. I had not anticipated that, and I had no money. I tried to convey this, apologized, and attempted to walk away. He followed me and continued to ask for money. I thought I could ask my parents but calculated that the odds that my dad would scold me—why had I taken the photo, how did I get myself involved in this?—were pretty high, and the young 10-year-old me was getting yelled at already. I was scared. The boy's cries went from imploring to inveighing against me. Next, he was pointing to me as he was yelling to his mother, who immediately came over and began gesticulating and yelling at me in Arabic. I did not understand one word she was saying, but it did not take much to figure out that she was not happy. I found our bus and got on, unsure of whether I had evaded them or not. I scurried to my seat. Was it over? But soon she was there, the mother. She had tracked me to my seat from outside the bus and was slapping my window with her hand and shouting very angrily at me. Forty-five years later, I remember this moment, the anger on her face, as if it were yesterday. My intent with this story is not to cast myself as some sort of victim. Of course,

I would come to understand that this poor boy, who had so little, felt that I, the privileged American, climbing back into my air-conditioned bus, had not held up my end of the deal. I remember wishing I could untake the photo. Could I somehow give back to him what I'd taken without even realizing it?

It was a frightening experience for me as a little boy. But it also was the beginning of an awakening. As if something, like a small stone deep in my being, had been shaken loose. It was one of my first direct encounters with poverty. I'd seen homeless people on the streets of New York City. Still, this felt much more like the desperation I had seen in late night television appeals by UNICEF but had never witnessed up close like this. Even more, it was my first unscripted encounter with a real Palestinian. While that interaction did not go well, I personally learned so much from it. I saw a boy, not much older than I, with so little. I saw a mom prepared to fight to protect her child's honor. I knew that my mom would do the same. Indeed, she had already.

My family kept this photo for many years. I think of it whenever asked about formative experiences. I remember it whenever I think of Jerusalem.

My Perceptions as a Young Adult

The second experience would be much later in my life, when I traveled for the first time to Jerusalem alone, as a young man in my twenties. My research as a graduate student took me to Jerusalem virtually every summer from 1990 to 1998. I was doing a PhD in Anthropology, with a concentration in Middle East Archaeology, which meant several weeks in the northern Negev at an excavation site and another month or so in Jerusalem processing our finds. It was among the first opportunities I'd had to venture far outside my conventional bubble. Almost immediately, I was seeing, hearing, and experiencing things that were not aligned with the narratives

I'd heard most of my life. Meeting real live Arabs, Palestinians, was exhilarating for me. In the shallowest sense, there was the excitement of risk. These were my so-called enemies, and I was testing boundaries, boundaries that had been set in my mind since my youth. The version of history I'd been taught in Hebrew school. The images created in cartoons, movies, and media.[49]

But the novelty of pushing boundaries did not last long, largely because you quickly realize and/or remind yourself that any built-in, baked-in boundaries between peoples are purely a social construct. People are people, and the possibility always exists for Christian and Muslim and Jew and anyone to make friends.

I note this because as a child, I was raised to believe that Jerusalem was for the Jewish people. It took multiple trips, and the chance to probe beyond my own narrow conception, to see a fuller picture of the holy city.

Another pivotal event in my life took place in Jerusalem in early 1996.

I arrived in late February of that year to serve as a Fellow at the W.F. Albright Institute. I lived at the Albright Institute in the heart of East Jerusalem, not far from the famous Damascus Gate of the Old City, while conducting research for my doctoral dissertation. My research was carried out in an archaeological laboratory in the French Centre National de la Recherche Scientifique (CNRS), involving the analysis of artifacts of one of the world's earliest metal industries. The ancient smiths had left behind the tools of their craft: ore, slag, crucibles, and furnaces. The material was excavated in the 1950s by a French archaeologist, but had never been analyzed or published, save for a few artifacts. Everything was arranged in advance—licenses, permissions, funding. It

49. Jack G. Shaheen, *Reel Bad Arabs: How Hollywood Vilifies a People*, 3rd Edition (Ithaca, NY: Olive Branch Press, 2012).

was a dissertation on a platter, and I was going to unlock the mysteries of the ancient metallurgists. I was excited about the research and enthusiastic about living for almost an entire year outside the U.S., in the Holy City of Jerusalem.

My first night there, an old friend invited me to a party in East Jerusalem, an area I had been warned, as an American Jew, to avoid. So, of course, I was all in. I met a roomful of super-cool, super-smart, sophisticated Palestinian twenty-somethings. It was in the years following Oslo, and there was still optimism in the air, hope for the prospects for peace. I was excited about all the new friends I'd made. But could this really be the case? Weren't these the very people I'd been told hated me, wanted to destroy me? But now, I was with real people, and not some imagined boogey man, and they embraced me, inviting me back. The next morning, while riding bus No. 18 to the lab, I recall thinking to myself, "What if more American and Israeli Jews met Palestinians like this? Could things be different?"

Tragically, the undoing of that optimism would begin to accelerate just days later, on February 25, 1996. Bus No. 18, the bus I'd been taking to and from the French Center every day since I had arrived, was attacked by a suicide bomber near the *takhana merkazit*, the Central Bus Station. Twenty-six people were dead and many more injured. My parents called: "Come home, it's not safe to be there." They knew I was riding the bus and offered to send money so I could take cabs instead. I assured them it would be okay. Lightning never strikes twice. Right?

The next day, February 26, there was another deadly suicide bombing at a hitchhiking post on the outskirts of Ashkelon. And on March 3, an unsettling second strike of lightning in the same spot, the second suicide bombing of Bus No. 18 on Jaffa Road in Jerusalem in one week. Nineteen people were dead. That day, I'd had some errands to run in my neighborhood before heading to the French Center and took a much later bus. Nothing seemed out of the ordinary to me as I boarded Bus No. 18 late that morning. But when I arrived at the Center, I quickly learned what had happened, and it sank in that the bus I'd been taking on a regular basis had become a target. The next day—March 4, 1996—just off Dizengoff Square in Tel Aviv, a suicide bomber detonated a 20-kilogram nail bomb. Thirteen people were dead, capping off one of the worst weeks of terror in the history of the conflict.

I spent the rest of that day just sitting in front of my assemblage of artifacts. It was as if I were staring at a table full of rocks. I couldn't focus, or rather, my mind was laser-focused, but not on my research. It felt as if our world were spinning out of control. And I just kept asking myself: is there anything at all I could do to contribute to solving this problem, even in the smallest way? And if there was, why wasn't I doing it? That afternoon, when I left the Center for the trek to East Jerusalem, my first thought, admittedly, was whether my Dad's offer to underwrite taxi transportation still stood. I understood that allowing the bombings to intimidate me was allowing the terrorists to win; but I certainly wasn't about to take the bus that day. As it were, finding my way home on foot that day was a critical piece of my journey. I got a lot of exercise in those next months, walking roughly one hour each way from the French Center to the Albright Institute. I had discovered an amazing route, walking "the *tayelet*," a massive promenade built of Jerusalem stone carved into the slopes facing east into the Jordan Valley. I also got a lot of thinking done on those walks through the neighborhoods of Jerusalem: Jewish Haredi neighborhoods, the Russian Quarter, Arab neighborhoods.

Recounting this story calls to mind Isaiah 2:3:

וְהָלְכוּ עַמִּים רַבִּים וְאָמְרוּ לְכוּ וְנַעֲלֶה אֶל־הַר־יְקֹוָק אֶל־בֵּית אֱלֹהֵי יַעֲקֹב
וְיֹרֵנוּ מִדְּרָכָיו וְנֵלְכָה בְּאֹרְחֹתָיו כִּי מִצִּיּוֹן תֵּצֵא תוֹרָה וּדְבַר־יְקֹוָק מִירוּשָׁלָם:

And the many peoples shall go and say:
"Come, let us go up to the Mount of the LORD,
To the House of the God of Jacob;
That He may instruct us in His ways,
And that we may walk in His paths."
For instruction shall come forth from Zion,
The word of the LORD from Jerusalem.

Present and Future

I don't believe in singular turning points—I am writing an entire book on this subject—but rather, I think people experience series of pivotal moments in life, when a certain groundwork has been laid over a long period of time, when there is a confluence of seemingly disconnected variables, and when a dramatic experience helps bring it all together, ultimately reaching our consciousness and finally our actions and deeds.

These were all critical moments in my journey: the boy with the goat, the evening with young, hopeful Palestinians, the week of terror attacks. It was all these Jerusalem encounters, and more, that moved me to a decision to do all that I could to advance peace in the region, to redirect my career in academia in the service of a common good, to become an academic in action. My own research and teaching would turn toward understanding sectarian violence, conflict resolution, and peacebuilding.

My first step would be a shift from the study of Jerusalem's past to Jerusalem's present. From studying the physical remains that ancient people left behind to understanding the love, hate, joy, and pain that the living souls of Jerusalem carry with them today. I delivered a conference paper and then published a book chapter titled, "Targeting Heritage: The Abuse of the Past in Conflicts of the Present." I wanted to understand how people use sacred space, what happens at the meeting point between past and present, and why so often holy sites become flashpoints for violence. As an anthropologist who studies religion, inter-religious dynamics, conflict resolution, and peacebuilding, I find sacred space fascinating, especially when it involves space to which multiple parties lay claim. How do we define sacred space, who gets to define it, how can we learn to live with one another even when we don't agree on all these questions? There is no more potent example of multiple parties laying claim to the same sacred space as Jerusalem.

As a Jew, a scholar, a peace practitioner, I have very mixed, complex views and feelings about Jerusalem. On the one hand, I grapple with the idea that this space is holier than others. I cannot as a Jew believe that God is limited to any one space or place. Rejecting the notion that the essence of God could be captured in stone—as in the scenario of Abraham in his father's idol shop—is one of the first developments in the evolution of Judaism.

Rabbinic scholars point out that in ancient times prominent voices expressed grave theological reservations about the idea of a fixed, earthly home for their deity.[50] Among those was the Priestly source, known simply as P, who insists that the peripatetic nature of the Tabernacle was quite intentional. Perhaps the strongest argument against the notion that God could be contained in a fixed, central place comes from the final chapter of Isaiah (66):

ישעיה סו:א כֹּה אָמַר יְ-הֹוָה הַשָּׁמַיִם כִּסְאִי וְהָאָרֶץ הֲדֹם רַגְלָי אֵי זֶה בַיִת אֲשֶׁר תִּבְנוּ לִי וְאֵי זֶה מָקוֹם מְנוּחָתִי.

Isa 66:1: Thus said the Lord: The heaven is My throne And the earth is My footstool: What house could you build for Me? What place could serve as My abode [lit. resting place]?

50. Rabbi Dr. Isaac S. D. Sassoon, "The Tabernacle: A Post-Exilic Polemic Against Rebuilding the Temple," *Torah.com* 2018, updated 2023; Terence Fretheim, "The Priestly Document: Anti-Temple?" *VT* 18 (1968): 313-329.

With all due respect to Jerusalem and the Western Wall, if I am honest, I've had more spiritually inspiring encounters with my faith experiencing the beauty of nature or interacting with fellow humans. I think of Shabbat services as a young teenager in the woods of my beloved Camp Ramah in Palmer, Massachusetts. On the other hand, there is no doubt that Jerusalem is one of the most spiritually uplifting places in the world. Jerusalem at sunset, with its long, purple shadows and soft magenta light reflecting off the marble-like Jerusalem stone, has this mysterious effect, as if the ground is bending beneath one's feet.

There is an old saying, in response to questions about this very point. "It's true that God can hear you anywhere you are. It's just that God hears it a little louder when you speak in Jerusalem." Today, many Jews and non-Jews who visit the Western Wall squeeze notes scrawled on small slips of paper into the thin cracks between the massive Roman stones of the wall's lower courses, believing their message is more likely to reach God.

So then, is this same hotline to heaven open to all people? Does God also hear the prayers of Muslims and Christians a little louder when they call from Jerusalem? It is not only Jewish souls that are stirred by this city. Jerusalem is home to the history and holy sites of multiple faiths and religious traditions. Jews, Christians, and Muslims from around the world come to Jerusalem. For many it is a pilgrimage, the word for which is a Hebrew-Arabic cognate *chag-hajj*. In the Babylonian Talmud (Megilla 26a) we are told that Jerusalem should be a city for all people: "Jerusalem was not apportioned to the tribes." Psalm 132 tells us that Jerusalem, specifically Zion, is the resting place of the Lord, while also affirming God's commitment to social justice in the city, a theme that receives an inspiring treatment in Rabbi Aryeh Cohen's *Justice in the*

City: An Argument from the Sources of Rabbinic Judaism.[51]
The Torah and Talmud also instruct us that no one person or
party can claim ownership of Jerusalem, precisely because it
belongs to no one, or it belongs to God. The Gospels echo this
same idea when Jesus quotes Isaiah (56:7): *He then taught
the people: "It is written in the Scriptures that God said, 'My
Temple will be called a house of prayer for the people of all
nations'"* (Mark 11:17). In the Qur'an, Surah 17:1, we read
that Muhammed journeyed by night "from the Sacred Mosque,
to the Farthest Mosque, whose precincts We have blessed, in
order to show him of Our wonders." The "Farthest Mosque,"
according to Hadith, is Al Aqsa, the silver-domed mosque
inside the 35-acre compound in Jerusalem, known to Muslims
as al-Haram al-Sharif, or the Noble Sanctuary. The text goes
on to reference God's message to Moses and Noah, prophets
of Judaism and Christianity, as well as Islam.

In the Jewish sources, nowhere is this message clearer than
in I Kings 8:41-43:

"וְגַם אֶל־הַנׇּכְרִי אֲשֶׁר לֹא־מֵעַמְּךָ יִשְׂרָאֵל הוּא וּבָא מֵאֶרֶץ רְחוֹקָה לְמַעַן
שְׁמֶךָ: כִּי יִשְׁמְעוּן אֶת־שִׁמְךָ הַגָּדוֹל וְאֶת־יָדְךָ הַחֲזָקָה וּזְרֹעֲךָ הַנְּטוּיָה וּבָא
וְהִתְפַּלֵּל אֶל־הַבַּיִת הַזֶּה: אַתָּה תִּשְׁמַע הַשָּׁמַיִם מְכוֹן שִׁבְתֶּךָ וְעָשִׂיתָ כְּכֹל
אֲשֶׁר־יִקְרָא אֵלֶיךָ הַנׇּכְרִי לְמַעַן יֵדְעוּן כָּל־עַמֵּי הָאָרֶץ אֶת־שְׁמֶךָ לְיִרְאָה אֹתְךָ
כְּעַמְּךָ יִשְׂרָאֵל:"

Also the foreigner who does not belong to Your people Israel
but comes from a distant land because of Your fame—for
they shall hear of Your great fame and Your strong hand
and arm outstretched—**when he comes and prays in this
house**, hear in heaven Your dwelling place and respond to
the call the foreigner makes to You so that all the nations of

51. Aryeh Cohen. *Justice in the City: An Argument from the Sources of Rabbinic
Judaism.* New Perspectives in Post-Rabbinic Judaism (Boston: Academic Studies
Press, 2012).

the earth may know Your name and worship [or fear] You like Your people Israel....[52]

A house of prayer for all nations, taken literally, probably sounds farfetched. But, in reality, there are tangible steps that can be taken today in the direction of this dream. Take the Haram al-Sharif/Temple Mount complex. The Western Wall is literally the western retaining wall of the monumental platform on which the holiest site to Jewish people, that of the First and Second Temples, stood, where stand today two of the holiest sites to Muslims, the Al-Aqsa Mosque and the Dome of the Rock. Tensions are always high in the area and violence often erupts. In the last two years alone, when Shavuot and then Passover coincided with Ramadan, there have been major clashes between Jewish and Muslim worshippers. Even within the Jewish faith there are disagreements over who controls sacred space at the Western Wall, especially when it comes to gender; in essence, there are Jewish men who exclude or marginalize Jewish women who seek to perform ritual activities at the site. Christians have fought each other so long over the Church of the Holy Sepulcher that Muslims, the famous Joudeh and Nusseibeh families, have been entrusted with holding the key.[53]

Short of a single, common house of prayer for all nations, distinct houses standing side-by-side in peaceful co-existence should not be an unreasonable goal. Hammering out the specific details of how people of all faiths can coordinate

---

52. This translation is provided in Rabbi Dr. Isaac S. D. Sassoon, *An Adventure in Torah: A Fresh Look Through a Traditional Lens* (Brooklyn, NY: KTAV Publishing House, 2022), p. 275.

53. Laurie I. Patton, "The Doorkeeper, the Choirboy, and the Singer of Psalms: Notes on Narratives of Pragmatic Pluralism in the Twenty-First Century," in C. Cornille and C. Conway (eds.), *Interreligious Hermeneutics* (Eugene, OR: Cascade Books, 2010): 228-249.

mutually respectful use of holy sites will not be easy. But it will become much easier when the parties can begin to build some measure of trust. Again, seemingly farfetched. But trust can be built on the shared recognition of holy space. Faith communities should not be dismissive of each other's seemingly competitive claims to sacred space; on the contrary, these claims are an affirmation that others acknowledge the sanctity of your holy space and maybe even some of your core beliefs.

As a Jew, I am thrilled that the Jewish people have returned to the city that has been sacred to our people for thousands of years. Jews the world over have yearned for Jerusalem in song, poetry, and prayer. As a Jew, I am also deeply saddened that Jewish renewal in the land has often meant the dispossession of others. In truth, virtually everyone in Jerusalem has lost something, again, the unfortunate result of zero-sum thinking that says for me to gain the other must lose, and vice versa. But this becomes a never-ending cycle in which even the winners lose.

There is no doubt that Jews belong in Jerusalem, but must that mean that Jerusalem belongs to Jews? Jewish return need not entail the erasure of others. If we all take a more magnanimous approach, we see that diverse claims to the city are not necessarily mutually exclusive. Presence without primacy.

Imagine, instead, if people of all faiths could co-exist, or better still, share the city. There is a solidarity dividend[54] to be earned, if we could all invest in even a minimal level of trust. A vital ingredient of trust is humility, and what could be more humbling than the walls of the eternal city, Jerusalem? To return to the opening question: yes, Jerusalem is in my heart, a heart that sings, cries, and prays for peace in Jerusalem.

---

54. Heather McGhee, *The Sum of Us: What Racism Costs Everyone and How We Can Prosper Together* (London: One World, 2021).

9.

The "Abandoned" Houses of Jerusalem
Tamar Verete-Zahavi

Jerusalem is my hometown. In this essay, I reflect on my early childhood there and try to reconstruct the process of understanding that once there were Arab inhabitants in West Jerusalem. They have left traces—beautiful houses and fruit-filled orchards. Who were these Arabs that had to escape from their properties? Were they my enemies? Was it moral to live in their "abandoned" houses? Would they come back? These many questions had built my political infrastructure as a young girl and as an adult. This essay is dedicated to my parents and grandparents who answered my questions patiently, seriously, and quite honestly.

When I was five or six years old, my parents were looking for a large flat for my grandparents and us. As time passed, I realized that this was a critical issue—if they don't find a large apartment, my beloved grandparents will have to move into a nursing home. The search for the apartment was not successful—it seemed that all of Jerusalem's apartments were found as *"rechush natoush*," which means "abandoned property." I didn't understand the meaning of these two strange and ugly words, but I felt that behind them there was a secret, one of too many secrets that the adults were keeping.

I was a sickly girl. I spent many days at home, with lots of time figuring out the grown-up world. These words *rechush natoush* reoccupied my thoughts. They were like the Latin names for bad diseases.

One might ask, why didn't I just ask my parents to explain these words to me? I guess I didn't because these topics of conversation were not for a young girl (like death, money, and sex). At best, I was allowed to listen to their conversations without interfering. That was one of the unspoken rules.

I associated the adjective *natoush* ("abandoned" or "neglected") with the small, abandoned kittens meowing in our backyard. Sometimes I tried to save them, but unfortunately, they all died. My mother explained to me that their mother had deserted them because they were sick and weak. I was very angry with these cruel cats, and I was a little bit afraid that I too might be abandoned if I were to get seriously ill. But what's the connection between poor kittens and large flats? I had no idea.

One Saturday morning when I was walking with my Dad, I discovered the meaning of *rechush natouch*.

It was a sunny morning, and we were walking hand-in-hand in our peaceful neighborhood of Rehavia. When we got to the unmentioned border between the Rehavia neighborhood and the Talbiya neighborhood, my father pointed to one of the houses. He said that my parents had intended to buy the large flat on the second floor, but that unfortunately turned out to be "*rechush natoush*." It was a beautiful building; in my child's eyes, it was like a small palace.

"What's wrong with the house?" I finally asked my dad, and he explained to me that until about fifteen years ago, Arab families were living in this house and in many houses in Jerusalem. During Israel's "War of Independence" (1948), many Arab families fled their homes because they were afraid of being hurt in the war (later I learned that many of them in fact were expelled from their houses).

"If the Arabs don't live here anymore, why can't you buy this beautiful apartment?" I asked him, and my daddy answered that he and Mummy feel uncomfortable living in a house that doesn't belong to them. I asked him if the meaning of *rechush natoush* is "stolen houses." He murmured something like—"Mmmm, the reality is much more complicated...." I asked him if Israel had confiscated their houses, as our teacher confiscates our toys if we play with them when she reads us stories. "It's kind of the same," he laughed. "But the teacher always returns the toys she confiscated. Would Israel return them their houses?" I was thinking out loud.

"I don't think so...but who knows...," my dad said.

"That's not right," I said. Looking back, I think that is when I realized that the natural justice had been violated. I was simply scared.

For many days I showered my dad with questions: Where are the Arabs that once lived in West Jerusalem? Did they take their furniture when they ran away? And their dogs and cats, did they leave them behind or did they take them along? Who lives in these houses now? Why hadn't Grandpa and Grandma run away during the war when, as Grandma had told me, there was no food and no water in Jerusalem at that time?

My dad, who was an historian, answered my questions with care. In retrospect, I know that these conversations weren't easy for him, and I really appreciate him for his courage.

On that Saturday morning, I lost my innocence. I suddenly realized that we, the Israeli Jews, are not "the good guys," as I had been told. That day my whole way of looking at Jerusalem, my hometown, was changed forever.

That's how I became a young urban geographer. Almost every afternoon I went with my Mum downtown. On our way, I would ask her about the history of the buildings that we saw. That is how I learned that my neighborhood, Rehavia, was built on property of the Greek Orthodox Church, and therefore the houses in Rehavia weren't *rechush natoush*. My mum continued to explain that the massive buildings in the center of Jerusalem (King George Street, Ben Yehuda Street, and Jaffa

Street) were "mandatories," which means that the British had built them and therefore, they also weren't considered *rechush natoush.*

But oops, how is it that a hundred meters from the central junction of Jerusalem there is a hidden abandoned mosque? What is this mosque doing there? Did those Arabs live here too? And the huge Muslim cemetery, also in the center of town, why did they bury their dead here? Why do we have to see signs of their faith everywhere? I felt that their houses, mosque, and tombs were evidence that something bad had happened in my hometown. I felt a heavy cloud lying on the city.

I would like to emphasize that these are not facts, but rather the way in which Jerusalem was constructed subjectively for me.

In retrospect, I believe that the information that my dad had given me about the Nakba (the Palestinian Catastrophe in 1948) in Jerusalem was quite a shock. I suddenly realized that life could change in one day. I realized that our stable daily life is reversible. The conversations about the *rechush natoush* were as frightening to me as were Grimms' Fairy Tales.

Walking with my Mum in the center of Jerusalem was like walking inside a fairytale. Downtown one could meet very strange people: dark-skinned Coptic priests, tall Russian Orthodox priests with their small ponytails, nuns of various orders, and of course, Orthodox Jews with their dark costumes and white socks (we didn't meet Palestinians in Jerusalem until the days after the June 1967 War). The exposure to social diversity intrigued me. I asked my Mum many questions about these people, coming from far away because of their belief that Jerusalem was holy.

I didn't really understand the meaning of "holiness," because we were a secular family, but I was thrilled to know that my hometown is important for people from all over the world. Because of their presence, I considered myself a native and thought of them as our guests.

One year later, after the 1967 war, when Israel had occupied East Jerusalem, the West Bank, and the Gaza Strip, I would consider the Palestinians as the genuine natives of this land, and my national identity would be cracked.

In looking back, I don't comprehend why as a young girl I was so preoccupied with these ethical, moral, and political issues. I'm quite sure that my friends weren't bothered by them. I believe that those issues threatened my wellbeing. Life seemed unstable to me.

Let's go back to my grandparents who lived not far from us, at 23 Gaza Street. Since my parents didn't find a suitable large flat, my grandparents had to move into a nursing home.

I clearly remember that before they moved out of their dark flat, my grandpa invited me to his local coffeehouse on Gaza Street. I was eating a hotdog, and he smoked a cigarette and drank tea. He explained to me what it meant that they would be moving to a nursing home and reassured me that I could visit them, and they would visit us. I asked him if the nursing home was far away, and he calmed me down, saying that Bus Number 7 would take Mummy and me to Hebron Road, and from there we would go down a narrow street to the nursing home at 52 Bethlehem Road.

I was curious to know the meaning of those names: Gaza, Hebron, and Bethlehem. (One year later, Israel had occupied these cities, and I could visit them.) My grandpa pointed his hand toward the west and said that if I had a donkey I could ride straight on, as he had done many years ago, and reach Gaza, an Arab town by the seashore. I imagined myself riding a sweet donkey while Grandpa kept explaining that with my donkey, I could ride all along the Bethlehem Road to the small Arab town of Bethlehem, and if we followed the Hebron Road we could visit Hebron, which is also an Arab town. Grandpa told me that before the War of Independence everyone could visit these lovely cities.

Wow, what a huge imaginary map was spread out in front of my child's eyes! Shortly after this conversation, my grandparents moved to 52 Bethlehem Road, to the nursing home that was in the *Baka* neighborhood. Till 1948 *Baka* was an Arab neighborhood. Almost every afternoon we visited my grandparents. On weekdays, my Mum and I took Bus Number 7, and on Saturdays we walked. When we got off the bus, I felt as if I was in another country. The architecture was different, especially near the nursing home, where one could see stone houses surrounded by beautiful fruit-filled basateen (or bustans) and orchards. In my neighborhood of Rehavia, I had only seen flower gardens, which were not very impressive, just for decoration. The bustans in Baka with their grapevine covered gazebos were mysterious and attractive. I remember myself imagining how nice it would be to sit on a stone bench in the middle of a *bustan* eating apricots or green grapes.

If you have read my words so far, you can imagine that I asked my parents and my grandparents dozens of questions about the families who had once lived in these houses and planted these orchards, and about the families living there now, who haven't planted these orchards but could now enjoy them.

I was told that when the Arabs ran away from their houses, new Jewish immigrants immediately entered these houses and became their owners. The new immigrants slept in the Arabs' beds, ate on their tables, and sat on their sofas. I remember how repulsed I was by those real stories. They reminded me of the story about Goldilocks and the three bears—I disliked this story too. How could Goldilocks sleep in the bears' bed, on their sheets? How could she eat from their plates with their spoons? As a privileged young girl, I couldn't identify with the suffering of the new immigrants, whose origins were from Arab countries, or refugees from the Holocaust. And my parents spared me and didn't tell me how miserable the new immigrants were.

I have finally succeeded at piecing together the information into a coherent picture: the Arabs who lived happily in Jerusalem had to leave their houses and orchards because of the big war. These Arabs weren't the "enemy"; they were nice people who just wanted to live their peaceful lives. The "enemy" in that war were the people from the villages all around Jerusalem, and the Jordanian legionnaires.

Once again, I want to emphasize that these are not historical facts; these are thoughts from my childhood.

There was no public transportation on Saturday, the Jewish holiday; therefore, we had to walk to my grandparents' place. The road was long but not tiring—our neighborhood, Rehavia, is on a hill, and *Baka*, which means "valley," lies at the bottom. On our way, we passed through the Talbiyeh neighborhood. I was always amazed by the majestic villas such as Villa Salameh, Villa Haroun El Rashid, and others. I asked myself who these rich people were. Who had lived in these villas? Did they have servants? Did a cook prepare their meals? Did they dance in ballrooms like princesses and princes? Walking through Talbiyeh's streets was like walking in a fairy tale.

I was seven years old when the "Six Day War" (1967) broke out. The Jordanians had bombed Jerusalem day and night. Houses around us were damaged. During these long days and nights, I certainly knew who our enemy was. I could imagine the Arabs and their red *Kuffiyehs* planning to throw us into the sea (that was the rhetoric we all heard). And I didn't know how to swim … and Jerusalem was far from the seashore. Would they take us by bus to the seashore and then throw us into the sea? All our family, including my grandparents, stayed together at home. My brothers and I got lots of candy and cookies, and we slept together on the hallway floor. The radio was on all day long announcing great victories. The Israeli army defeated five Arab states that wanted to destroy us. I felt relief; we were saved. It was the first time I sensed national pride! I remember my dad and grandpa launching glasses of wine when the Old City of Jerusalem was taken by Israeli soldiers. Their eyes shone with tears.

A few weeks later, we visited the "Holy Basin," in the Old City of Jerusalem, for the first time. We passed through the immense Jaffa Gate and entered the old market, the *shuk*. I can't find the words to describe the beauty of this market. The Arab merchants were kind and smiling. I asked myself, "How come they are 'The Enemy'?" Everything was cheap. We entered a grocery store; all the products were new to me. Suddenly I saw something familiar—Kit Kat, my favorite chocolate, which our dad had brought us from England! I was sure this chocolate was the most expensive and rare in the world. How could it be that I have found this treasure in the *shuk*?

And there were donkeys, my favorite animals, and even camels, sheep, and goats. The Old City of Jerusalem, a 25-minute walk from our home, became our favorite place. We had delicious foods. We walked around these winding alleys and discovered new things every time. The Old City was like heaven on earth for me.

The occupation of Palestine (we still didn't call the victory an "occupation," and we didn't yet name the occupied territories—Palestine) influenced our daily life: Mahmoud from Hebron was our gardener and Souheila from Bethlehem was our cleaning lady. They came every day to Jerusalem by bus. The supermarket delivery guy was Arab. My Mum always offered him a glass of cold water. The laundry workers were Arabs, as well as the street cleaners. One can say that we were surrounded by Arabs … and they were very nice people, far from being enemies.

My mental map of Jerusalem had suddenly changed. I couldn't connect the absent Arabs of *Talbiyeh*, *Baka*, and *Katamon* (West Jerusalem) to the Arabs of the Old City (East Jerusalem). But slowly, slowly they appeared, the Arabs of 1948 or their relatives. I heard my parents talking about them: they came from Ramallah, from Nablus, from Jordan, and even from the United States, to visit their "abandoned" houses. According to the Israeli Absentee Property Law, they couldn't even buy their own houses back; they could only visit them if the Jewish residents let them. Although I was an eight-year-old girl, I could see the whole complicated picture, and I began to understand the recent complicated history of my hometown.

10.
"Go West": Reflections on the "West" in West Jerusalem
Elan Ezrachi

My father was born in Jerusalem on April 1, 1925. On that day, another iconic event took place in another part of the city: the opening ceremony of Hebrew University. My father, *Eitan*, was born in the newly settled modern Jewish neighborhood of *Rehavia* located in West Jerusalem. According to our family records, he was the first baby boy who was born in the neighborhood that had sprung up just a year before. Those three benchmarks: the founding of Hebrew University, the birth of my father, and the founding of *Rehavia* frame my essay.

Let's go back a few years. In 1911, my father's father, Shmuel Brisker, left Odessa and sailed to Jaffa. He was 23 years old and an active Zionist. Unlike most of his Jewish contemporaries who were emigrating from Eastern Europe to the United States, he chose to go to Palestine. After arriving in Jaffa, he moved to Jerusalem, a place he never left until his death in 1969. Soon after his arrival, he was joined by Bella Temkin, his girlfriend from Odessa. They got married in Jerusalem and started their journey as a family. One feature of their journey was to change their name into a Hebrew name: Ezrachi.

My grandparents were secular modernist Eastern European Jews. By the time they had arrived in Jerusalem, there was a very small modernist community present in the city. Most of the Jews in Jerusalem at the time were traditional-Orthodox, representing the 'old' (pre-Zionist) community of Jews that had lived in the city for centuries. Still, my grandparents found a small group of like-minded people who chose to live in the city that was governed by the Ottoman Empire. Their community was the nucleus of what would later become modern West Jerusalem.

World War I wreaked havoc in Jerusalem. Many residents, Jews and Arabs, were deported or ran away. The city was in shambles; those who remained suffered from dire physical hardships. My grandparents, like many others, were forced to leave the city and were exiled to Tiberias in the Galilee. In December 1917, the fate of Jerusalem changed dramatically when the British army conquered the city and marked the beginning of a new era. Shortly after, my grandparents returned to Jerusalem. At first, the British had to restore basic living conditions but soon afterwards they midwifed a glorious chapter that transformed Jerusalem into a modern city. In 1920, the British military administration was replaced by a civil system paving the way for further progress. This status remained until May 1948, when the British Mandate ended.

During the British rule of Jerusalem, the city's visual image and character were radically altered, as well as its geographical and demographic dimensions. While the British did not build many monumental buildings themselves,[55] they were catalysts for a robust process of urban planning and development. They set new planning guidelines that shaped the look of the city for the years to come. Already in 1918, they brought a city planner, architect William McLean, the Alexandria city-engineer, and commissioned him to draft a new masterplan for the city. Urban planning was an entirely new concept for the city that until then had evolved without clear guidelines. McLean's concept was to move the city toward the west and keep the Old City

55. There were several exceptions, including the main post office, the residence of the high commissioner, and the Rockefeller Museum. But, as a general rule, most of the construction was done by local initiatives.

separate, as a protected heritage site. Around the same time, Ronald Storrs, the British governor of Jerusalem, established the Pro-Jerusalem Society, a civil organization aimed to ensure that Jerusalem would develop according to strict guidelines that would preserve its beauty and significance. Several other planners came after McLean, among them Professor Patrick Geddes, who participated in the planning of Tel Aviv. Those plans and the actual developments that followed them had a clear Western-modernist orientation.[56]

The British invested tremendous efforts in the development of Jerusalem. Once the Old City was defined as a heritage site, the westward sprawl began. The developing New City was part of Jerusalem, but it also had a distinct Western character, with a feel of a different city. The British planning codes were strictly modern and Western-oriented. They facilitated specific neighborhood masterplans that shaped the character of the new city. Those plans included zoning of private and public land uses; supervision of construction quality and the requirement that all building facades use natural limestone.[57] In short, Jerusalem under the British rule went through a radical transformation that has influenced its character until this very day.

Where were the Jews in the transformation of Jerusalem? In the early days of Zionism, there was ambivalence toward the place of Jerusalem in the Zionist enterprise. When the Zionists imagined their project, they saw new agricultural settlements and modern cities along the coastline. Hence, the Kibbutz and Tel Aviv were signature features of the Zionist activity. Jerusalem had an image of an antiquated, religious,

---

56. Gideon Biger, "The Contribution of the British Rule to the Development of Jerusalem in its first Years," *Studies in the Geography of the Land of Israel*, 1976, Vol. 9, pp.175-200.

57. "Jerusalem—The Capital of the British Government of Palestine, 1917-1948" in Aviva Halamish, *Jerusalem Throughout the Ages, Unit 10: Jerusalem during the British Mandate*, pp. 17-19.

and conflicted site—images that secular Zionists were keen to avoid. The arrival of the British changed this ambivalence. The British policy regarding the centrality of Jerusalem pushed the Zionist leadership to focus on Jerusalem and develop it as its future political center. In the 1920s it was already clear that Jerusalem would be the political hub of the Zionist project.

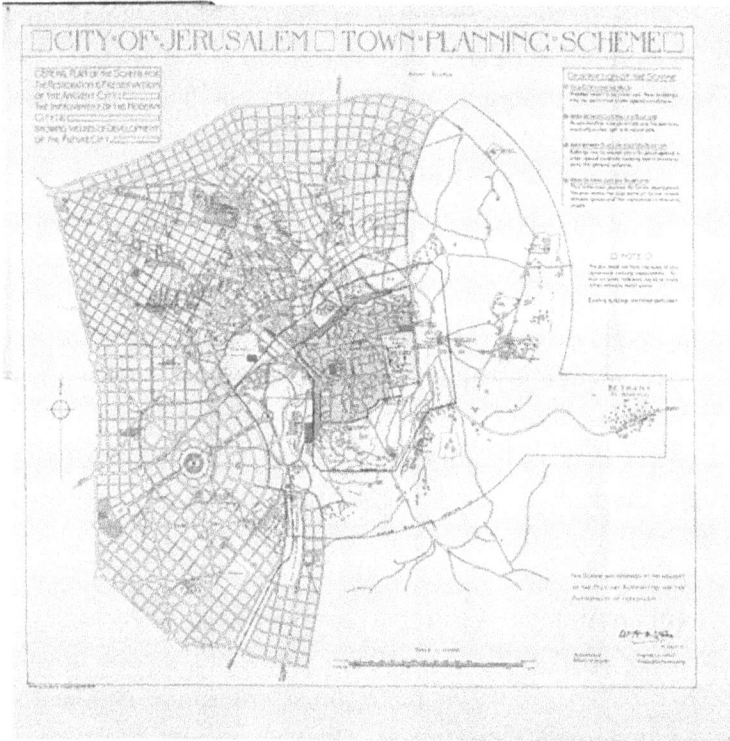

McLean's Plan of 1918, depicting the move toward the west

One of the key expressions was the construction of the headquarters of the central national institutions in Jerusalem on King George Street.[58] The headquarters compound was built in the heart of the new city, adjacent to the newly built *Rehavia* neighborhood. The opening of Hebrew University

58. The Central National Institutions included the World Zionist Organization, the Jewish Agency for Israel, the Jewish National Fund, and Keren Ha'Yesod.

in 1925 added another dimension of Western culture within the Jerusalem landscape. The University was designed with strong European academic codes. Though the campus was in the eastern part of the city (on Mt. Scopus), the faculty and students came mostly from the rapidly developing western side. The new University, as well as the newly-built Hadassah Hospital, the National Library, the central Zionist organizations, and the new commercial center—all served as opportunities for new Jewish migration that came into the city. Thousands of European Jews who immigrated to Palestine during those years found their home in a developing modern city: West Jerusalem.

Together with the development of the new western city center and the aforementioned public buildings, the period of the 1920s saw massive development of new Jewish residential neighborhoods. Here, again, the Zionists were proactive. They purchased massive lands from declining Christian institutions (primarily the Greek Orthodox Church). During the British Mandate era around 40 Jewish neighborhoods were built. Most of them were quiet suburban developments with one-story, village-like homes. The Zionists invited a German-trained architect, Richard Kauffmann, to oversee the project. Kauffmann was known for planning many sites all over Palestine, and most famously the six *garden suburbs* of Jerusalem. "Garden Suburb" was a style that was popular in England in the 1920s. The Garden Suburbs were a new modern direction in the urban culture of Jerusalem. They became home to the Hebrew University faculty, medical doctors, professionals, and leaders of the Zionist movement. *Rehavia* was the most famous neighborhood in this trend. A parallel process occurred among the Arab community. Well-to-do Arabs also built new and elegant neighborhoods, among them, Musrara, Talbia, Katamon, Baka, and Abu Tor.

The new Jewish neighborhoods had all the features of modernity: detailed masterplans, modern infrastructure, private homes with gardens, Hebrew street names, lighting, public transportation, communal facilities (schools, synagogues), in short, a modern urban concept. My grandparents bought a lot in *Rehavia* and built one of the first homes in 1924. My father grew up in *Rehavia*, the new neighborhood that possessed a European feel and look. Most of the residents of those neighborhoods had a European education and lifestyle. Hebrew was my father's first language, and that was the main language that was spoken in the Jewish sections of West Jerusalem. The immigrant parents spoke other European languages: Russian, Polish, German, and/or Yiddish, but their children were raised on Hebrew. My father attended the famous modern Gymnasia School, and in the afternoon hours he was part of a Zionist youth movement. As most others of that community, he did not speak a word of Arabic, and as a secular person he had no reasons to visit the holy sites in the Old City. Like many of his generation, when he graduated high school, he left Jerusalem to establish a new Kibbutz in the north. Several years later, he returned to Jerusalem to attend Hebrew University.

The British who ruled the city for 31 years allowed the Jewish and Arab communities to develop, each side with its cultural and religious integrity. Jews and Arabs lived side-by-side in a mixed city with clear ethnic, cultural, and religious dividing lines. Aside from a few exceptions, Jerusalem was essentially a mosaic of separate Jewish and Arab neighborhoods.

At the end of 1947, the situation in Jerusalem changed dramatically. After the United Nations resolution of November 29, a war broke out between the Jewish and Arab communities all over Palestine. This war quickly spilled into the confines of Jerusalem.[59] The City, which was once an integrated urban

---

59. This war had several names, based on the beholder. The Israelis call it the War of Independence, others call it the 1948 War.

unit, became the battlefield between the local Jewish and Palestinian communities that were present in all parts of the city. Each side strived to gain control of significant strategic, political, and religious sites. In May 1948, the State of Israel was declared, and the Palestinians in Jerusalem were reinforced by the Jordanian Legion. As was described earlier, the Jewish community of Jerusalem was mostly located in the western part of the city. However, the roads leading to Jerusalem from the west were controlled by Palestinians and, as a result, the Jewish community of Jerusalem was under a harsh siege for several months. The Israeli forces struggled to break the siege and restore the connection between the Jews of Jerusalem and the rest of the newly declared country. They succeeded in this endeavor but stopped short of taking over the entire city to include the Old City.

This essay does not intend to cover the details of the battle over Jerusalem. Suffice it to say that the War of 1948 resulted in the division of the city. In November 1948, the two sides[60] agreed to draw a line that defined two distinct neighboring cities. West Jerusalem was under Israeli control, and East Jerusalem was under the control of the Hashemite Kingdom of Jordan.[61] The dividing line reflected, for the most part, the demographic reality that existed prior to the War. Before 1948, most Jews resided in West Jerusalem, and therefore they remained in their homes. A small minority of Jews who lived in East Jerusalem, primarily in the Old City, were forced to move to the Western side.[62] On the Palestinian side, a more significant number of individuals and families lived in West

---

60. By now, one side was Israel, and the other side was Jordan.

61. One exception was Mt. Scopus, a site in East Jerusalem that remained as an Israeli enclave with restricted access to it. The site that was the home of Hebrew University and Hadassah Hospital became inaccessible to the two institutions.

62. The largest group of residents of the Jewish Quarter of Old City had been forced to move earlier, in May 1948, after a fierce battle.

Jerusalem and because of the War they lost their homes and moved elsewhere.[63]

From this point, the term *West Jerusalem* gained two new connotations: first, it was the site of the Capital of the newly established State of Israel. Shortly after the end of the War, Israel declared West Jerusalem as the Capital of the young country.[64] Israel swiftly placed its central bodies in the city: The Knesset (Parliament), government offices, Supreme Court, and national memorial sites. Second, the term "West Jerusalem" now held a new geopolitical meaning; it was the part of Jerusalem that was under full Israeli control. The other part was in the hands of a different country. And above all— West Jerusalem was entirely Jewish.[65]

While the division of Jerusalem was somewhat of a defeat for the Israeli side, it served as an opportunity to invest further in the development of West Jerusalem, a trend that had begun during the British era. In addition to the institutional development, the government of Israel settled large numbers of new Jewish immigrants who were migrating to Israel after 1948. Many of them were settled in new public housing projects that were swiftly built for them, mostly toward the southwest.

I was born into this city in 1955. All my childhood images and memories were rooted in Israeli West Jerusalem. The West Jerusalem of my childhood was a relatively small town, with under 100,000 residents in 1949 and 200,000 in 1967. The

---

63. See Adnan Abdelrazek, *The Arab Architectural Renaissance in the Western Part of Occupied Jerusalem* (Cyprus: Rimal Books, 2017).

64. This declaration in December 1949 came after a United Nations decision that announced Jerusalem as an internationally controlled city. Israelis defied that resolution and went on to actualize their decision to define Jerusalem as Capital.

65. There was one exception: part of the Palestinian village of Beit Safafa in the south of Jerusalem remained in the Israeli side and its residents became part of Jerusalem.

population in West Jerusalem lived either in the Jewish and (now empty) Palestinian neighborhoods that were built before 1948, or in the new immigrants' housing projects that were added to the west of the veteran neighborhoods. The British western downtown that was created prior to 1948 became the main city-center of Israeli West Jerusalem.

When we wanted to get away from our immediate surroundings, there were two diametrically opposed options: going toward the east meant facing an international border. It was both dangerous and exciting. There were warning signs, barbed wires, and mined areas as well as occasional cases of sniper shooting. But going toward the border was also exciting as we could peek into the other side.

The other option was going toward the west, and that meant getting away from the border and being absorbed in the images of the developing western city. West of our homes there were distinctly modern images: the new campus of Hebrew University, the monumental Knesset (Parliament) building, Mt. Herzl, the Israel Museum, wide parks, and even a European-style pine tree forest. And if we wanted to leave the city, the only open exit route was to the west, toward Tel Aviv.

The term West Jerusalem of my growing up meant several things. First, it was that part of Jerusalem over which Israel could assert its control. It also meant that there is a part of Jerusalem that was not under Israel's control and not within its reach. Second, there was the yearning to end this liminal stage and connect to the other side, primarily to the sites that were important to Jews. Third, West Jerusalem was also a stand-alone city.

The National Convention Center, 1958

Israel's National Library Building, 1960

The clear image of West Jerusalem ended abruptly in June 1967. It happened quickly as a result of the Six Day War. On June 7, only 48 hours after the war erupted, Israel conquered all parts of East Jerusalem, and shortly afterwards, the entire

West Bank was under Israeli control. The stunning military conquest set the stage for a new Israeli narrative: United Jerusalem. East and West Jerusalem would now need a new framing. They were no longer two cities, side-by-side, divided by an international border.

Two weeks after the war ended, the Israeli government announced new municipal boundaries for the city. The new city limits included all sections of the Jordanian city as well as surrounding areas that were populated with small Arab villages. Israeli law was extended to these new boundaries. The Palestinians who were living in those newly added areas received the status of permanent residents of Israel. The walls that separated the two cities were quickly removed, and once again, Jerusalem was one urban universe. Jews and Arabs who had been separated for 19 years were again residents of one city that would now be governed by one administration. This time, the city was not controlled by an outside force, i.e., the British, but by Israel, the dominant power. And this Jerusalem was much larger than any prior definition of the city.

For me, as an adolescent growing up in the western (Israeli) side, the unification was a very exciting change. A new and exotic city that had been hidden behind a wall was revealed. Within walking distance from my home, I could experience other languages, cultures, historical and religious sites, enchanting markets, and human diversity. But this honeymoon was short-lived. As time went by, it became clear that the unification of Jerusalem was a forced artificial maneuver. The international community did not recognize the unilateral Israeli decision, and the Palestinians of Jerusalem saw themselves as a community under occupation. Israel asserted its rule by massive building all over East Jerusalem, settling Jews in the newly added areas. New roads, archeological excavations, a new national holiday (*Yom Yerushalayim*), naming streets and sites in Hebrew—all were aimed at creating an irreversible reality. Jerusalem became the heart of the Palestinian-Israeli dispute.

What happened to the concept of West Jerusalem? Did it retain its significance? In many ways, the term lost its meaning. West Jerusalem as a modern, Western-oriented, secular, Israeli urban space was no longer the lead narrative of Jerusalem. Israelis turned their attention eastward with the focus on intensification of the unification narrative. Jerusalem today is more religious, more conflicted, and its future is amorphous. The residents of Jerusalem are insulated from each other in their discrete religious and ethnic communities. They tend to focus on their daily lives. Perhaps the dominant narrative is survival until the next chapter.

Still, to me, the term West Jerusalem is not completely lost. It represents the vision of what Jerusalem can be. It is my story, and I would like to see this story continued. As a community activist, I believe that there is a tremendous vitality in the city and there are many groups and communities that wish to restore the idea that Jerusalem is a liberal, Western-oriented place and not a site of controversy and dispute.

References

Abdelrazek, Adnan. *The Arab Architectural Renaissance in the Western Part of Occupied Jerusalem.* Cyprus: Rimal Books, 2017.

Ben-Arieh, Yehoshua. *The New Jewish Jerusalem in the Mandate Period (1917-1948): Neighborhoods, Houses, People* (Hebrew Edition). Jerusalem: Yad Ben-Zvi, 2012.

Benvenisti, Meron. *Jerusalem, the Torn City.* Minneapolis, MN: Minnesota University Press, 1976.

Biger, Gideon. "Early British Contributions to the Development of Jerusalem, 1918-1925." *Mehkarim Begeagrafiyah shel Eretz Yisrael* 9 (1976): 175-200 (Hebrew).

Elon, Amos. *Jerusalem: City of Mirrors.* London: Little, Brown and Company, 1989.

Ezrachi, Elan. *Awakened Dream: 5o Years of Complex Unification of Jerusalem* (in Hebrew). Herzlia, Israel: Albatros, 2017.

Halamish, Aviva. *Jerusalem Throughout the Ages, Unit 10: Jerusalem during the British Mandate*, Second Edition (in Hebrew). Ra'anana, Israel: Open University Books, 2020.

Schmeltz, Uziel O. *Modern Jerusalem's Demographic Evolution.* Jerusalem: Magnes Press, 1987.

Segev, Tom. *One Palestine, Complete: Jews and Arabs under the British Mandate.* London: MacMillan, 2000.

11.

O Jerusalem: Reflections of a Liberal Zionist on the Too-Holy City
Ilan Peleg

Exactly fifty years ago, in 1972, two journalists, Larry Collins and Dominique Lapierre, published a massive, 572-page book under the title of *O Jerusalem*. The international bestseller describes the events that led to the establishment of Israel in 1948, focusing on the war over Jerusalem. The publication of the book, just five years after the 1967 Six-Day War, was an important event in emphasizing the intensity of the conflict between Arabs and Jews over Palestine/Israel, focusing appropriately on the holy city of Jerusalem as the emotional center of people on both sides of the deep national and religious divide.

In the wake of Collins and Lapierre, this essay, written from the perspective that I would define as moderate, liberal, and Zionist, promotes an argument comprising several components. First, I will describe the moderate Zionist position on the centrality of Jerusalem compared to the centrality of other places in Eretz Israel and the symbolic values that might be associated with them. Second, an analysis of the changes in the dominant Zionist perspective on Jerusalem brought about by the 1967 War will be offered, highlighting the emergence in Israel of a particularistic perspective associated with the Zionist Right and the subsequent marginalization of a more universalist perspective that has been present in traditional Zionist thought and action from its beginning. Third, I will describe the actual policies (which I characterize as "triumphalist") adopted by successive Israeli governments and City administrations toward Jerusalem, dwelling on their consequences in creating an ever more divided rather than a more united Jerusalem. Fourth, the essay will present an alternative policy to the one implemented by most Israeli administrations since 1967, a policy reflecting the values brought to this discussion by this author—pursuing justice in Jerusalem, the "City of Peace,"[66] as well as adopting a position reflected in the Biblical commandment of "Justice, Justice thou shalt pursue."[67]

Alternative Zionisms

From the very beginning, the Zionist movement has witnessed the development of different variants of its vision for a future Jewish state. Of particular interest for this essay is to recognize that one version of Zionism was open to the idea that there were other interests in Palestine in addition to Jewish interest in establishing political presence in the land.[68] It is also important to recognize that along with this fundamentally compromising position on the part of the majority of Zionists, there has been from the start a minority Zionist position that has been considerably more radical, claiming the entire country as an exclusive Jewish patrimony. The stark difference between these two alternative positions was reflected in their responses

---

66. The etymology of Jerusalem as "the City of Peace" is one of several possibilities.

67. "Justice, Justice thou shalt pursue," Deuteronomy 16:20. This central principle is reflected also in Ruth Bader Ginsburg and Amanda L. Tyler, *Justice, Justice Thou Shalt Pursue: A Life's Work Fighting for a More Perfect Union*, 5th ed. (Berkeley, CA: University of California Press, 2021).

68. Those other interests were already recognized in the iconic, foundational Balfour Declaration of November 2, 1917, a declaration issued by the British Government and, importantly, incorporated in the Mandate given to Britain by the League of Nations in 1922.

to a series of proposals to partition the land between Arabs and Jews (e.g., in 1922, 1937, and 1947).

This territorial debate within the Zionist movement reflected an even deeper debate between Universalists and Particularists, with the former promoting social or liberal democracy and the latter promoting a nationalist, territorialist, and militarist agenda. This internal conflict has evolved since the 1967 war into a genuine *Kulturkampf* (cultural war).[69]

The universalist-particularistic debate within the Zionist movement was reflected in different perceptions of Jerusalem: on the one side, what could be identified as the particularistic Nationalist Right, and, on the other, much more universalist Labor Zionism and middle-class liberal centrists. Among some Zionists, there was an attempt to create alternative secular "holy" places to Jerusalem's Temple Mount in order for Zionism to detach itself from messianic sentiments,[70] and, I would argue, to blunt the evolving conflict with the Arabs. Places such as the Jezreel Valley, Masada, and the campus of the Hebrew University were promoted as alternative sacred sites. This project of establishing alternative national symbolism failed, especially following and as a result of the 1967 war.

Moreover, in addition to seeking alternatives to Jerusalem, it is important to note that even within the Jewish religious tradition, Jerusalem in general and the Temple Mount in particular have been open to both universalistic and particularistic emphases, perspectives, and interpretations. Thus, the universalistic Jewish tradition focuses on the Temple

---

69. See Ilan Peleg, "The Peace Process and Israel's Political Kulturkampf," in Ilan Peleg, ed., *The Middle East Peace Process: Interdisciplinary Perspectives* (Albany, NY: State University of New York Press, 1998), 237-63.

70. See Hillel Cohen, "The Temple Mount/al-Aqsa in Zionist and Palestinian National Consciousness: A Comparative View," *Israel Studies Review*, Vol. 32, no. 1 (Summer 2017): 1-19.

Mount's Foundation Stone as the very place from which the creation of the world began, implying that "all human beings [and not only Jews—I.P.] have a link to the place."[71] In the prophetic tradition of the ancient Israelites, this universalistic outlook is expressed, for example, in Isaiah's utopian vision: "In the days to come, the Mount of the Lord's House shall stand firm above the mountains…and all the nations will flow to it."[72]

Needless to say, side by side with a universalist perspective on Jerusalem, a more particularistic tradition among Jews in regard to the city has been in existence for millennia. The two ancient temples stood on Temple Mount, both David and Solomon ruled from Jerusalem, and the city is referred to in practically all Jewish prayers. The immigration of Jews to Eretz Israel and specifically to Jerusalem eventually made them into the majority in the city.[73] The important fact that ought to be recognized in the context of this essay, however, is the inherent duality in the perception of Jews and particularly Zionists toward Jerusalem and especially the Temple Mount. According to Hillel Cohen, for most Jewish immigrants to Israel/Palestine in the critical era between 1882 and 1923, "Jerusalem became secondary, even on the symbolic level" within the Zionist ethos, a position promoted by prominent Zionist leaders such as Berl Katznelson and future Israel's president Chaim Weizmann.[74] Moreover, during the 19 years of Jordanian occupation of the Old City and all of East Jerusalem (May 1948-June 1967), Hillel Cohen characterizes

---

71. Ibid, 9.

72. Isaiah 2:2.

73. For detailed analysis of the demographics of Jerusalem, see Michael Dumper, *The Politics of Jerusalem Since 1967* (New York: Columbia University Press, 1997), especially Chapter 3.

74. Cohen, "The Temple Mount/al Aqsa," 12.

Israeli attitude toward the Temple Mount as "ideological disengagement," a period in which the holy site "disappeared from Israeli consciousness."[75] From my perspective, Cohen's description is not only entirely accurate but, in terms of future policy, also serves as a key for a better future for the city and the region.

The 1967 War and
the Rise of Israeli Nationalist Particularism

The 1967 war changed the geographic and the geopolitical balance of power in the Middle East. Most important was the transformation among many Israeli Jews about the acquisition of additional land in general and changing the status of Jerusalem in particular. The immediate result of the conquest of the West Bank, including East Jerusalem and the Old City, was the restoration of dormant Israeli ambitions regarding total control over all of Jerusalem. The 1967 war unleashed powerful nationalist forces within Israel, forces that would make future accommodation in regard to Jerusalem unlikely to materialize.

Nevertheless, the annexationist forces within Israel were not unchallenged, despite the powerful, post-1967, nationalist euphoria in the country. In fact, some of the most prominent political leaders understood from the very beginning the necessity for controlling Israel's national appetite, particularly in its religious-messianic manifestations, and especially regarding the Temple Mount. Thus, Minister of Defense Moshe Dayan, the single most popular Israeli leader in the post-1967 War era, instituted immediately following the conquest of all of Jerusalem a policy that, while allowing Jews to visit the Temple Mount as tourists, banned them from holding religious

---

75. Cohen, ibid., 13.

services there. Furthermore, Dayan left the administration of the Temple Mount in the hands of the Muslim Waqf, while approving the demolition of the houses in front of the Western Wall. Dayan and the rest of the post-1967 Israeli government, of which he was a senior member, were pursuing a moderate policy of compromise, taking into account the interests of both Jews and Muslims in regard to the most sensitive venue in Israel/Palestine, Jerusalem's Temple Mount.

Yet, nationalist forces in Israel, particularly religious ones, began immediately after the June 1967 war to push for complete Israeli control over the whole of Jerusalem, including the most sensitive area of all, the Temple Mount. The battle over Jerusalem has shifted quickly from the military arena, where Israel defeated Jordan in short order during the 1967 war, to the political arena, where the Israeli nationalist-annexationist Right has battled against the more moderate Center-Left over the specific policy toward occupied East Jerusalem and toward the Temple Mount. The Jerusalem issue quickly emerged within the Israeli polity as an important religious and political one.[76]

Since 1967, Right-wing Israeli individuals and groups have been pushing for ideas designed to wreck the status quo—the administration of the Temple Mount by Muslims (specifically, the Waqf) and the Western Wall by Jews (specifically, Israel's Chief Rabbinate). One policy change advocated by some within the Israeli Religious Right has been allowing Jewish prayers on the Mount. Another idea, a lot more radical, has been the rebuilding of a Jewish prayer venue—a synagogue or even the erection of the Temple—at this most sensitive of all places. It is important to note that the internal debate among Israeli Jews over the appropriate demands regarding the holy site is not simply between religious and secular Jews,

76. Marshall J. Breger, "Religion and Politics in Israel," *Journal of International Affairs*, Vol. 50, no. 1 (Summer 1996): 90-118, especially 91.

but between moderates and radicals within Israel's religious camp. Thus, among Orthodox Jews there has been for a long time a prohibition against prayer on the Temple Mount and even visiting it, let alone rebuilding the Temple there.

The prolonged but inconclusive peace process in the Middle East, rather than generating optimism among Israeli Jews in the hope that the multi-generational conflict might be soon concluded, often rekindled the controversy between Israeli hawks and Israeli doves over the future of the Temple Mount. The seemingly successful Oslo Accords of 1993 and the subsequent negotiations at Camp David in the summer of 2000, for example, intensified the internal Israeli debate over the future of the Temple Mount. Helena Cobban observed in 1994 that "what happens in Jerusalem…will be a major factor, perhaps the major factor, in determining whether the peace process…can stay on the rails."[77] Her observation is still valid today.

Overall, the hawkish Israeli position on Jerusalem seems to have been strengthened through the years, contributing significantly to the difficulty of reaching an Israeli-Palestinian agreement. At the same time, it should be emphasized that the position of Palestinian negotiators regarding Jerusalem in general and the Temple Mount in particular, including that of PLO Chairman and PA President Yasser Arafat, has been just as uncompromising as the position of hawkish Israelis.

The non-compromising position on the Israeli Right has been advanced by both secular nationalists and nationalist-religious circles opposed to a final peace deal between Israel and the Palestinians. Nationalists of all stripes know full well that in the absence of an agreement on the future of Jerusalem and the Temple Mount, there cannot be a final settlement of the Israeli-Palestinian conflict. Thus, the most important Right-

---

77. Helena Cobban, "U.S. Policy on the Issue of Jerusalem," *Jerusalem: A Special Report* (Washington, DC: Center for Policy Analysis on Palestine, 1994), 30.

wing party, the Likud, ran its 1996 electoral campaign under the banner of "Peres will divide Jerusalem,"[78] an accusation repeated on many other occasions. But the vanguard of Israeli radicalism on the question of the Temple Mount has always been in the hands of Nationalist-religious circles. Thus, for example, the number of rabbis[79] who support Jewish visits to and even prayer sessions on the Mount has been on the rise. What might be thought of as the sanctification of the site by religious authorities is undoubtedly a major obstacle to finding a compromise solution at present and in the future.

Hillel Cohen believes that "the Temple Mount is a place in which the Zionist national and Jewish religious discourse come together."[80] In agreeing with Cohen's description, it is my conviction that the interaction between nationalism and religiosity among Israelis, as among Palestinians, has created over the last several decades unfavorable conditions for progress toward both peace and justice in the Holy Land. Religion, especially in its extremist variants, breeds irrational and absolute demands that are not conducive to compromise solutions of politically complicated conflicts. In this sense, the shift of many Israelis from the essentially rational policy of Dayan in 1967 to the religiously based demand to conduct Jewish prayer on Temple Mount and even erect there the Third Temple has proven to be highly unhelpful.

---

78. The accusation was directed at Labor's candidate, Prime Minister Shimon Peres.

79. Such as Yisrael Ariel, Chaim Drukman, and Dov Lior. In 1996, a rabbinical council of the West Bank ruled that it is permissible to visit the Temple Mount, contradicting a long-established ban on doing so. See Judah Ari Gross, "Fighting rabbinic ban, Jewish activists push Temple Mount prayer toward mainstream," *Times of Israel*, June 2, 2022.

80. Cohen, "The Temple Mount/al Aqsa," 15.

The Policies of Triumphalism in "United" Jerusalem

While Jerusalem is often viewed, particularly from the outside, as a sacred city with renowned holy sites such as the Temple Mount, or Haram-al-Sharif, the Wailing or Western Wall, the Church of the Holy Sepulchre and the Via Dolorosa, it is also demographically a medium-size city with politically enormous problems. The religious character of Jerusalem, along with its nationalist centrality, makes a solution to its dilemmas extremely difficult. Moreover, the determination of Israeli governments, particularly on the Right, to put a "united Jerusalem" at the very center of the country's national identity has turned this triumphalist position into the major barrier to a rational solution to the Israeli-Palestinian conflict.[81]

Since 1967, Jerusalem has become for both Israelis and Palestinians a primary symbol for achieving their nationalist aspirations. As such, it has emerged as a bone of contention between the Israeli Right and the Israeli Left and between radical and moderate Palestinians. In the case of Israel, the public and political debate has been between those who support a "united Jerusalem" under Israel's exclusive control and those who adopt a more moderate stance, willing to recognize that non-Jews have also legitimate interests in the City. The nationalists believe that all of Jerusalem must be eternally the capital of Israel and never the capital of another nation or state. Their perception of what is the area of Jerusalem includes the Old City and East Jerusalem. Among the Palestinians, the nationalist demand is for the inclusion of the Old City, and particularly the Haram al-Sharif, in the future Palestinian state and for the establishment of Jerusalem as the capital of that state. The prominent Palestinian position and the nationalist

---

81. Some analysts believe that the Israeli focus on Jerusalem led to Jerusalem becoming "more important in Palestinian political and economic consciousness"; see Breger, "Religion and Politics in Israel," 103.

variant of the Israeli position are incompatible and cannot lead to a compromise solution. However, a more moderate Israeli position, along with an equivalent moderate Palestinian position, could lead us toward a "Jerusalemite Compromise" that is essential to an overall peaceful solution to the Israeli-Palestinian conflict.

While the fundamental goal of Israeli policy, particularly under Right-wing governments, has been the establishment of a united Jerusalem under an exclusive Israeli control and formal annexation, in reality the story of Jerusalem has been "a tale of two cities," in conflict with each other, one dominating the other. The time has come to recognize this reality as a first step toward a better future for all the City's inhabitants.

The Peace and Justice Alternative:
Liberal, Zionist, and Realist

Among many early Zionists there were significant speculations that Tel Aviv, a new city reflective of the spirit of Jewish renewal, might emerge as the capital of the future Jewish state. Moreover, the Mandatory power Great Britain (1937), and later the international community through the UN General Assembly (1947), envisioned Jerusalem as a city under international control.[82] Be that as it may, upon its establishment, Israel built its capital in West Jerusalem, and during the 1967 war it conquered the rest of the city. This unexpected occupation of Jerusalem and the West Bank created new political dynamics in the State of Israel, reflecting a messianic, religious spirit in Israel, a reality that made peace with the Arabs—in Jerusalem and in Israel/Palestine—difficult and possibly unachievable.

---

82. Moreover, even "Ben-Gurion and other Founders implicitly accepted the internationalization of Jerusalem as the price of independence for some part of Palestine," and several alternative capitals were considered in a December 1947 meeting of the Jewish Agency (Breger, ibid., 101).

Several weeks after the 1967 war, the Knesset expanded the boundaries of Jerusalem to include all East Jerusalem, the part of the city that prior to the 1967 war was part of the Hashemite Kingdom of Jordan.

At the same time, 55 years after the legal unification of Jerusalem, the prospect for stable and peaceful life within the city is unpromising despite the legal action by the Knesset: (a) First, there are still hundreds of thousands of Muslim and Christian Palestinians living in Jerusalem; (b) the Palestinian national movement, representing at least partially this population, envisions at least East Jerusalem, inhabited by Arabs, as the future capital of a Palestinian state; (c) while Jerusalem is at the very center of Jewish national and surely religious identity, it is equally part and parcel of Palestinian identity, including the identity of Palestinians and other Muslims who do not live in Jerusalem; and (d) while the annexation of East Jerusalem might be the cornerstone of the identity of most religious-nationalists in Israel, it is not necessarily the essence of the identity of more liberal and democratic Israelis. These alternative and competing national-religious identities within Jerusalem suggest that there ought to be a serious examination of the possibility for a compromise between Israeli-Jewish interests and Palestinian-Arab interests in order to achieve peace and justice in this ancient, sacred city, and possibly in the country as a whole.

It is my belief that the only way of solving the complicated Jerusalem problem is through a combination of three factors: Moderation, Wisdom, and Imagination. Moderation requires a balanced approach that considers the national and religious interests of all parties rather than promoting a "solution" based on the interests of only one side. Wisdom calls for the designing of realistic and implementable solutions, not an idealistic and unworkable one. Imagination means creativity, thinking outside of the box in dealing with the Jerusalem issue.

The goal of a moderate, wise, and imaginative solution for Jerusalem is to bring to the city both peace and justice. Peace requires a solution that both sides—Israelis and Palestinians—can accept, not because it gives them all they want but because it gives them the most important things they want; for peace to be sustained, we need a formula that combines the minimally acceptable conditions for both sides. For justice, we need a formula that is seen by the parties to this conflict as responding to their desires. The current situation in Jerusalem does not meet these conditions, nor is there a serious process designed to generate these conditions.

In devising a solution for the overwhelmingly complicated Jerusalem dilemma and the holy sites within Jerusalem, a few principles ought to be recognized:

1. Jerusalem and its holy sites do not "belong" to one side alone: there is a multiplicity of interests that ought to be considered in devising a solution acceptable to the various parties, sold by the negotiating leaders to their people, and implemented in good faith.[83]

2. In devising a solution, one has to recognize that the different faith communities with interests in Jerusalem—Jews, Christians, and Muslims—are not homogenous. Thus, among Muslims, the Palestinians are but one party. Others, such as the Jordanian Hashemites, also have long-term and profound interests in the future of Jerusalem.

3. Specific sacred sites such as the Temple Mount, the Western Wall, or the Church of the Holy Sepulchre should be accessible to all people, regardless of

83. The tragic fate of other complicated settlements such as the Versailles Treaty ought to serve as a warning against an agreement that the parties or many publics within them resent.

their religion and regardless of who administers the site. There should be no limitations on the right of pilgrimage to all.

4. Administration of the various sites will require special arrangements, given that some sites (primarily the Temple Mount) are sacred to more than one religion or to different denominations within one religion (primarily the Church of the Holy Sepulchre). If there are multiple interests in a sacred site, an interfaith committee that includes representatives of the various groups should be established, possibly chaired by an impartial UN representative.[84] While this provision does not amount to the internationalization of Jerusalem, it incorporates the idea that the international community has an interest in at least certain sites within Jerusalem.

5. The holy places in Jerusalem should enjoy all international protections and guarantees included in the appropriate agreements, including the 1972 UNESCO Convention Concerning the Protection of the World Cultural and Natural Heritage and the 1954 Hague Convention for the Protection of Cultural Goods in the Case of Armed Conflict.

6. A particularly important and sensitive issue that ought to be resolved is that of providing guarantees for access to Jerusalem itself, not merely access to the holy sites within Jerusalem. Closures instituted by the Israeli authorities from time to time have hindered various groups—particularly Muslims in Israel and in the occupied West Bank—from reaching the City

---

84. Such proposals have been circulating in the past, often endorsed by the main protagonists. See, for example, Michael Parks, "Israel Suggests Shared Control of Holy Sites," *Jerusalem Post* (July 20, 1994), 1; Walid Khalidi, "Thinking the Unthinkable: A Sovereign Palestinian State," *Foreign Policy*, Vol. 56, no. 4 (1978): 706.

on particularly important days (such as Fridays) or for sacred observances (such as Ramadan). Such closures should be limited to the bare minimum and, to the extent possible, coordinated by all pertinent constituencies.

7. The overall settlement of Jerusalem should be based on the establishment of divided sovereignty, as recommended by both several (albeit by no means all) Israelis and Palestinians.[85] The idea is simple, logical, and realistic: Jewish neighborhoods in Jerusalem will be under Israeli sovereignty, and Arab neighborhoods will be under Palestinian sovereignty, a principle included also in the Clinton Parameters of late 2000. In general, Israel will control West Jerusalem, and Palestine will control East Jerusalem. The status of the Israeli neighborhoods in East Jerusalem will be determined in Israeli-Palestinian negotiations on the final geographical status of the West Bank, of which East Jerusalem is part. It is important to note that while sovereignty will be divided, under no circumstance should the city be physically divided.[86]

8. The Israeli and the Palestinian "boroughs" within Jerusalem should have maximal powers in essentially localized areas of governmental activity such as education, building, zoning, welfare, and the like; they should enjoy full autonomy. Areas that require cooperation between the boroughs, such as transportation and security, should be handled by what Professor Shimon Shamir called a "metropolitan

85. On shared sovereignty, see Mark A. Heller and Sari Nusseibeh, *No Trumpets, No Drums: A Two-State Settlement of the Israeli-Palestinian Conflict* (New York: Hill and Wang, 1991), especially 114-124.

86. The experience with divided cities—Berlin, Nicosia, Trieste and pre-1967 Jerusalem itself—has been quite negative.

roof municipality."[87] Both communities should be represented at the roof municipality.

9. In summation, the model offered here will enable Israel and Palestine to have their capitals in different parts of Jerusalem, while enabling the metropolitan area to function smoothly as a united city. Each holy site will be governed by the community that views it as sacred, unless a particular site is holy to more than one religion or denomination, in which case it will be governed by interfaith committees (as specified in Clause 4 above). The principle on which this proposal is based is to promote divided sovereignty for both Israelis and Palestinians as much as possible and to avoid shared sovereignty (given the long-term inter-communal hostility). When coordination is required—as in holy sites that are sacred to different communities—interfaith committees with the participation of international representatives will be established to have a mechanism for solving conflicts in an authoritative manner.

In devising an agreement on Jerusalem, as part of a larger agreement on Israeli-Palestinian peace, it is essential to be politically realistic. Political Realism in today's situation—56 years after all of Jerusalem was conquered by Israel—means the acceptance of a few self-evident facts with relevance for an agreed-upon, negotiated settlement. First, no Israeli government, regardless of its moderation, is likely to "return" all East Jerusalem to Arab rule, given that the city has been under Israeli control for a long time and that, if anything, Israel has moved to the Right since at least 2001, with religious nationalism heavily represented in its governmental

87. See "Shimon Shamir outlines his Jerusalem plan to Maariv," *Mideast Mirror* 8, no. 96 (May 20, 1994), as reported in Breger, "Religion and Politics in Israel," 106.

institutions. Second, any proposal for a physical re-division of the city is bound to fail due to fierce Israeli opposition to it. Third, no Muslim, whether Palestinian or not, will accept the "loss" of Muslim control of the Haram al-Sharif (and the same goes for the Christian position on the Church of the Holy Sepulchre or the Jewish position on the Western Wall). So, the recognition of these various interests is the *sine qua non* of any realistic proposal.

Yet, even with these absolute restrictions, red lines if you will, I believe that a negotiated solution is not merely highly desirable but possible. We know that during a few phases of the so-called peace process, solutions for Jerusalem, including the holy sites, were seriously discussed by Israelis and Palestinians. What is needed is an unshakable commitment to peace, a realistic position on what is really possible, and innovative/imaginative thinking in order to produce such a solution.

While I have no doubt that the solution presented here responds to the requirements for establishing a just solution to one of most difficult conflicts in modern history, I do not underestimate the inherent difficulties in reaching the type of solution I offer here, and the equivalent challenge in selling the agreement to the relevant national publics and eventually implementing the agreement.

Nevertheless, Jerusalem, among the most precious jewels created by humankind, deserves a sincere effort by the parties to the conflict and by the international community. While the goal of such effort should be to maximize justice, this could only be done by a creative process that is also cognizant of the difficulties in the real world.

12.
My Jerusalem—Our Jerusalem
Sharon Rosen

Jerusalem has been an indelible part of my identity since my earliest memories. I was weaned on its significance although its enormous influence on my life was my father's doing. More of that later. Growing up in a privileged home in North-West London, England, within a vibrant and highly homogenous Jewish environment, I could not have enjoyed a more secure setting, both socially and economically. Yet, at the same time, I knew through osmosis, even before I was able to articulate it, that I had two powerful and inextricably linked parts to my identity: I was British and Jewish and proud to be both. Born five years after Israel's miraculous independence as a Jewish state that seemingly rose like a phoenix from the ashes of the European concentration camps, my Jewishness manifested as Zionism, a love of Judaism as a religion, as a people, and as a nation that had returned to its ancient homeland.

I was born into a Modern-Orthodox family, imbibing the cultural and social pleasures of a vibrant London amidst a post-World War II boom and a cosseting Jewish community that had not been ravaged by the antisemitism that almost destroyed Judaism in Europe. Even though my father volunteered as a soldier in the British army during World War II and was incarcerated as a prisoner of war, first in Italy and then in Germany for several years, he and everyone else I knew at that time never spoke about those war years. We looked forward, not back.

My parents were members of Mizrachi,[88] a global religious Zionist movement, and I remember as a small child them opening our home for large fundraising events for Israel. My early education at a Jewish elementary school reinforced this love of Israel, whose pinnacle was Jerusalem. I prayed every day facing east toward Jerusalem, calling for its restoration in the central prayer of our services.[89] I engrossed myself in the narratives of the Torah,[90] and through its storytelling, enhanced by the experiential and symbolic enactment of the Jewish pilgrim festivals three times a year, I imagined that I too had been on a journey through the desert for forty years from slavery in ancient Egypt to freedom in the Promised Land. I felt the pain of the great prophets, Isaiah and Jeremiah, describing the woeful destruction of the Temples, first in 586 BCE, and then in 70 CE with its concomitant exile from Jerusalem two thousand years ago. However, those vivid and formative stories also spoke of the promise of a glorious return and a messianic redemption.

From the age of eleven I fasted 25 hours annually[91] to commemorate the Temple's destruction, sang songs about Jerusalem's hills and golden vistas, and vicariously lived the life of a pioneering Israeli from the comfort of my London home. This dual identity was perhaps best exemplified by the prayers read out by the rabbi every Sabbath morning in synagogue when we all stood to attention. Immediately following the prayer for the welfare of Queen Elizabeth II and

88. https://mizrachi.org/mission/.

89. 14th blessing in the weekday "Amidah" (standing, silent, prayer): *And to Jerusalem your city return in mercy and dwell in her midst as you have spoken, and (re)construct her speedily in our days, (re)built for eternity, and (re)establish the seat of David, your servant within her; Blessed are You who (re)builds Jerusalem.*

90. The five books of Moses comprising the first main section of the Hebrew Bible.

91. Fast of the 9th Av in the Jewish calendar when no consumption of food or drink is permitted among other restrictions.

all the Royal Family, we prayed for the welfare of the State of Israel and its defense forces. The rabbi intoned: "And may we be worthy in our days to witness the fulfillment of the word of Your servants, the prophets, 'For out of Zion shall go forth the Law and the word of the Lord from Jerusalem.'"[92]

If home and school were formative influences on my life, the third leg of the triangular stool on which I was raised was the Bnei Akiva Religious Zionist youth movement whose weekly meetings I attended for six years and which absorbed my free time and my mind.[93] At the end of every meeting, we sang Israel's national anthem, "Hatikva."

> As long as the Jewish spirit is yearning deep in the heart, with eyes turned toward the East, looking toward Zion, Then our hope—the two-thousand-year-old hope—will not be lost: to be a free people in our land, the land of Zion and Jerusalem.[94]

This was immediately followed by the Bnei Akiva anthem, "Yad Achim,"[95] calling on us to go "forward to the heights" of our homeland, the holy land of our fathers.

By the time I visited Israel for the first time in 1966, the die was cast—I was in love with a country that could not have been more different from my actual birthplace, England. Driving up to Jerusalem and seeing it suddenly appear on the hills in all its light and majesty (in those days there was no contiguous building stretching out from the holy city to the west), my tears flowed and for many years thereafter my heart would skip a beat every time I saw it on the horizon. As

92. Isaiah 2:3.

93. The children (sons) of Rabbi Akiva (translation from Hebrew).

94. "Hope" (translation from Hebrew).

95. "Brotherly Hand" (translation from Hebrew).

our sages declared in the Talmud, "Ten measures of beauty came down to the world; Jerusalem took nine,"[96] and "He who has not seen Jerusalem in its glory has not seen a truly beautiful city in his life."[97] The beauty of Jerusalem for those weaned on its awe-inspiring Jewish significance is clearly not just a physical beauty but a deeply spiritual one as well. In fact, Jewish tradition ascribes seventy names to Jerusalem—including Zion—attesting to her overarching meaning for the Jewish people.

On my first visit to Israel, before the 1967 Arab Israeli war, Jerusalem was cut in two, West and East, with Jews forbidden from visiting their holy site, the Western Wall (or Wailing Wall, as it was known then) in the Old City of East Jerusalem, which at that time was under Jordanian rule. I remember standing tiptoe on a large stone at the Mandelbaum Gate, the checkpoint dividing the city, trying to imagine the Wall just behind the hill and the large tree blocking my view! I could catch a glimpse of the magnificent gold-plated Dome of the Rock on the Temple Mount/Al-Aqsa Compound, the Jewish people's most holy site and from which sanctity emanates outwards, but, knowing that rabbis for hundreds of years had forbidden Jews from setting foot on its sanctified ground, I did not imagine visiting it.[98]

When I visited Jerusalem again in 1968, I marveled at the transformation. Suddenly all its vistas were open to me. The year before, Israel had powerfully won the war in less than a week against its Arab enemies, and the whole city was now

---

96. Talmud Bavli Kiddushin 49b.

97. Talmud Bavli Succah 51b.

98. This prohibition was reiterated by the Chief Rabbis of Israel Yonah Metzger and Shlomo Amar, and significant rabbinical figures associated with the national religious world, who issued a halakhic (Jewish law) ruling in 2005 against Jews entering any part of the Temple Mount "in our times." A similar ruling was issued several months after the Six Day War in 1967. Reported in *Ha'aretz*, January 18, 2005.

in the palm of its hand, including Judaism's most holy site. I remember visiting the Western Wall with great emotion, shopping in the markets of the Old City, and traveling from there on an Arab bus to visit the Cave of Machpela[99] in Hebron, a journey I shared with some sheep who were taking a shortcut led by their shepherd—quite a sight for a London city girl!

With the seemingly enhanced security situation in Israel after the 1967 war, my father made a decision that had enormous ramifications on my life. He declared that the whole family was making "aliya,"[100] emigrating to Israel, after he had wound up his business. This was an era of obedience toward fathers, but he did not need to persuade me. I had been well indoctrinated and was excited by the idea of playing my part in this new phase of the Jewish people's living history. Decades later, we found out why my father was so insistent that we leave our comfortable home, community, and cultural life in London for the sands, heat, and guns of Israel. When we finally prevailed upon him to relate his World War II experiences, he told of his escape from the German prison camp and how he had passed by the Theresienstadt concentration camp as it was being liberated. The sights he saw there left an indelible impression, and he swore to himself that if a State of Israel was ever established, he would make it his home. After 1967, he thought it safe enough to emigrate without putting his family in physical danger. Thus, in the summer of 1970, I flew to Israel to start a new chapter of my life with a certainty that it would play out in Jerusalem.

For the first three years, I studied at the prestigious Hebrew University, Jerusalem. Initially I lived on Mount Scopus in prefabricated huts that were an excuse for student housing, but

---

99. Hebrew name for The Tomb of the Patriarchs: Abraham, Isaac, and Jacob, and their wives. See Genesis 23.

100. Literally "going up," with a meaning that all Jews going to live in Israel are elevating themselves spiritually.

the excitement was palpable as buildings were sprouting up rapidly on the Mount to transform it into the main university campus after it had been out of bounds for Israelis from 1948 to 1967 as a UN-protected exclave within territory administered by Jordan. We students used to take the Palestinian bus from Mount Scopus and cross over the Mount of Olives to the Old City, where we would be welcomed with open arms by the Palestinian traders selling their wares. During those euphoric years, as my love affair with Jerusalem continued, I studied at the university's West Jerusalem campus on Givat Ram although I was to return to the magnificent Mount Scopus campus in later years to study for a postgraduate degree. It was exhilarating to live in a place where I truly felt at home, where I could live my Jewish way of life and not have to explain why I needed to leave school or work early on a Friday afternoon to prepare for the Sabbath, or be absent on a Jewish festival; where I could find synagogues at every turn; where kosher food was ubiquitous; and where Hebrew, the language of the Bible, prevailed.

I was mixing in exclusively Jewish circles, naively unaware of the undercurrents of political tension apart from a violent attack now and then which Israel seemed to have under control. In my third year, I met the love of my life, an army chaplain at the time based at the Suez Canal on the border with Egypt, but even his experiences did not hint at the impending violence of the October 1973 Arab-Israeli war. However, by the time war broke out, we had married and left for South Africa, where we served Jewish communities for six years, after which we continued to Ireland for a further five years. It was not until January 1985 that I returned to Jerusalem with three children in tow, older and wiser.

Living in apartheid South Africa and in Ireland during the Troubles,[101] and witnessing the oppression of people in both places simply because of their race, color, or ethnic background, focused my mind on the universal, theological message at the very start of the Torah, at the very heart of a person's connection to God—that EVERY human being is created in the Divine image.[102]

Returning to Israel and to my beloved Jerusalem, I saw the country with new eyes. Instead of only seeing the state as a Jewish miracle and the first flowering of Jewish redemption, I opened my eyes to another people living on the land, Palestinians, who also hold it dear. I began to ask myself, "What does it mean for two peoples to find the same land holy, to feel this umbilical attachment, and how can we find a way to live together without violent conflict?" Particularly in Jerusalem, where more than a third of this extraordinary city is Palestinian and where Islam's third most holy site casts its aura, it gradually became clear to me that brandishing the message of exclusive ownership cannot be a solution to ending violence. The question for me then became, "Is there a way for us all to feel a sense of belonging to this city without insisting on exclusivity?" And in religious terms, "How do I live the call found in Judaism to seek peace and pursue it?"[103] What was my role in all this?

The transformation within me was not immediate. It was a process of awakening, particularly as I knew little about Palestinians and their national aspirations. That had not been a part of my early formative education! However, I was

---

101. The Northern Ireland nationalist/sectarian conflict continued for over thirty years. I lived in Ireland during a high level of violence in the early 1980s when Irish Republican prisoners were dying on hunger strike in the Maze prison.

102. Genesis 1:21-27.

103. Psalm 34:14.

fortunate that life, or perhaps Divine guidance, has directed me on this path of discovery. I returned to post-graduate studies and befriended Palestinians in my classes, learning about their lives and dreams. Following my studies, I co-founded and directed an educational foundation providing life-skills to students and teachers in kindergartens and schools in Israel, which then branched out to Palestinian schools in the West Bank.[104] These experiences prepared me for a new role that I was offered in the Israeli/Palestinian, Jerusalem office of Search for Common Ground (Search), the largest international organization dedicated to peacebuilding, which has been my professional home for the past seventeen years.

Looking back on my years in South Africa, I could not have imagined any other end to the apartheid regime except a bloody revolution that would eventually overthrow it. And yet Nelson Mandela was released from Robben Island by President F.W. de Klerk and through strength of character and a commitment to dialogue, was able to bring about non-violent democratic change in his country. When I was living in Ireland in the early 1980s, an end to the violence that had continued for hundreds of years seemed impossible. And yet in recollection, we know it was the power of grassroots dialogue and the building of trust across enemy lines that enabled the political leaders to find a way forward to a cessation of violence with the Good Friday Agreement.[105]

I joined Search's office, located in East Jerusalem, in January 2005, inspired by those seismic non-violent changes in South Africa and Ireland, and as the Second Intifada was

---

104. Education for Life Foundation provided life-skills in communication, mediation, meditation, and understanding human diversity.

105. The Good Friday Agreement, which brought an end to the violence, was signed by United Kingdom, Ireland, and Northern Ireland's political parties in April 1998.

gasping its final violent breaths.[106] Living in Jerusalem during the Intifada, I was enormously grateful that, despite some very close shaves, my family and I were alive and unharmed, although others I knew were less fortunate. However, despite the slogans bandied about by Israeli politicians of an eternal capital of the State of Israel never to be divided, Jerusalem's wounds were bleeding, and the city's residents were as divided as ever and deeply traumatized. The holy city, sacred to the three Abrahamic faiths, Judaism, Christianity, and Islam, was also deeply divided by its faiths. We would have to pull ourselves up from the rock bottom we had reached and start building connections inter-religiously and across ethnic divides if we were going to create the fertile ground needed for a sustained political solution to the conflict.

With this in mind, my first role at Search was to direct a Holy Sites Initiative whose specific goal was to engage regional religious and political leaders in a process to reduce tensions around Jerusalem's highly contentious and volatile holy sites, which arguably were and continue to be the fulcrum for the periodic violent explosions we experience in the region.[107] The project's objective was to unite religious leaders, with the tacit approval of their respective governments, in a public declaration that formally acknowledged and respected the attachments of each of the Abrahamic faiths to their holy sites and to set up a mechanism to prevent future conflagrations around religiously sensitive issues. It was an attempt to galvanize the power of interreligious peacebuilding at a time when religion was seen as the problem, not the solution. While the Israeli-Palestinian conflict is first and foremost about two peoples' attachments to

106. Also known as the Al Aqsa Intifada, this was a violent Palestinian uprising against Israel from September 2000 to February 2005.

107. In addition to Al Aqsa being the lightning rod for the explosive start to the Second Intifada, a further example is the Israeli-Gaza war in May 2021, which was sparked by tensions at the Al Aqsa compound.

the same small piece of real estate, the conflict over the years has become more and more "religionized," with the flames of violence being stoked by people's fear that their deeply held religious identities are being attacked and delegitimized. As a result, Jerusalem, beloved by billions, is the crucible from which those flames emanate. How extraordinary it would be if the Psalmist's call for the peace of Jerusalem prevailed instead, and if all who loved her would be secure![108]

From the perspective of today's situation on the Al-Aqsa Compound/Temple Mount, the initiative was clearly a spectacular failure although it did have an initially promising start.[109] I ask myself whether I was too ambitious in going "straight for the jugular," to the most sensitive location of the conflict, in my belief that people in conflict can still find ways to collaborate on issues of common interest. Or did it fail because impeding political and personal interests too often get in the way? In this case, outside influences played a heavy hand, including the success of Hamas in the 2006 Palestinian national elections followed by Israel's incursion into Gaza in 2008,[110] which resulted in Palestinian President Mahmoud Abbas's freeze on all cooperation between Israelis and Palestinians, an anti-normalization policy that is still in place today. As American historian Barbara Tuchman points out, governments repeatedly pursue policies that are contrary to their interests.[111] Nevertheless, it is also clear that if we do not

---

108. Psalm 122.

109. Sharon Rosen, "Search for Common Ground: The Importance of Interfaith Cooperation for the Protection of Jerusalem's Holy Sites" in *Sacred Space in Israel and Palestine: Religion and Politics*, edited by Marshall J. Breger, Yitzhak Reiter, and Leonard Hammer (London, New York: Routledge, 2012), Chapter 11.

110. Israel's "Operation Cast Lead," incursion into Gaza ended with a joint ceasefire after three weeks in January 2009.

111. Barbara Tuchman, *The March of Folly: From Troy to Vietnam* (New York: Knopf, 1984), 4.

audaciously and tenaciously pursue initiatives like these, we are destined to live out a less well-known saying of our ancient Jewish sages that followed their statement about Jerusalem's beauty: "Ten portions of pain came down to the world, nine to Jerusalem and one to the rest of the world."[112]

The work on the Holy Sites Initiative was, however, not in vain, and by an interesting and exciting turn of events it returned to Jerusalem in another format to reduce interreligious tensions at the shared holy site, The Room of the Last Supper and King David's/Nebi Daoud's tomb on Mount Zion, just outside the Old City's walls, where over two million pilgrims visit annually. The experience I garnered from the Holy Sites Initiative was integrated into a *Universal Code of Conduct on Holy Sites*[113] that I developed together with representatives from three other international non-governmental organizations, and which has been endorsed by senior religious leaders of all faiths worldwide. It has also been implemented successfully in countries from Nigeria to Bosnia-Herzegovina as well as Mount Zion. The Universal Code's purpose is to safeguard holy sites from attack and enable adherents to access freely and to pray at their sacred spaces. But, at its heart, it promotes the message that holy sites can truly be protected only if all relevant authorities, including religious leaders, use a collaborative and supportive approach that builds and sustains trust, as opposed to a dictatorial one. Sadly though, we are witness to the absolutely contrary behavior at the most sensitive and significant of Jerusalem's Holy Sites. Until the present approach changes, Jerusalem will never live up to the prophet Zacharia's messianic vision of a restored city serving a universal destiny as a global center of pilgrimage and celebration.[114]

---

112. Talmud Bavli Kiddushin 49b.

113. https://www.codeonholysites.org/.

114. Zechariah 8:22.

I have lived in Jerusalem for over forty years, and for the last seventeen I have been privileged to overlook its Old City. I hear the muezzin call, the bells ring from the neighboring convent, and the Jewish prayers from the park opposite my home. Jerusalem is a city of beauty, of pain, and of Messianic potential to be a beacon of light and peace to the billions who hold it dear. Its three-thousand-year turbulent history[115] attests both to the city's tenacity and to human faith. I hear it calling me to grasp hope by the horns and continue building paths to peace so that Jerusalem can reach its potential and be the joy of the whole world.[116]

---

115. See Simon Sebag Montefiore, *Jerusalem: The Biography*, revised version (London, UK: Orion Publishing, 2020).

116. Psalm 48:3.

13.

Jerusalem: An Insider/Resident's and Outsider/ Researcher's Perspectives
Menachem Klein

Jerusalem: Real versus Imagined

I was not born in Jerusalem but have lived there most of my life. I was brought to the city. My parents moved to Jerusalem when I was about five years old. Since then, over sixty years, Jerusalem has been my permanent place for residency. During this long period, my academic career brought me to live half a year or a whole year in other cities: three times in London, twice in Oxford, and once in each of Florence, Leiden, and Cambridge, Massachusetts. Thus, my perspective on Jerusalem is of an insider who compares it to other places.

My resident's perspective is different from that of a tourist or visitor who enters Jerusalem from outside and returns to his or her home place. Jerusalem's holy sites, as well as its oriental bazaars, historical sites, stone buildings, and multi-religious population, attract tourists and visitors. Many of those who visit the city from outside have imagined it prior to walking in its streets. Holy texts, preachers, stories, poems, and media reports build up their imagined Jerusalem. In most cases, they come to see their imagined Jerusalem "in reality." Very rarely the real city takes the place of the imagined city as their dominant perception.

Geographically, the imagined Jerusalem is limited to the Old City and its immediate environs. Prophets, kings, pilgrims, crusaders, and defenders fill its streets, churches, mosques, and the Jewish Temple. Overall, in the three monotheistic religions, Jerusalem is not an earthly place but heaven's gate. Jerusalemites' everyday life experience is different. As I drive in the city, I do not meet prophets, except those infected by the "Jerusalem Syndrome." Instead, I deal with broken roads and traffic jams. Very often, I have to change my route because of a political demonstration, the convoy of a foreign head of state, or a violent clash between Israeli Jews and Palestinians.

The real Jerusalem is spread much beyond the Old City. It is the largest city in Israel in both territorial size and population. Never in history was the city so big. Its boundaries run around 126 sq. km., encompassing almost one million people, of whom 38 percent are Palestinians. Following the June 1967 War, Israel unilaterally created these boundaries in violation of international law. Since then, Israel changed the city's infrastructure unprecedentedly and developed its Jewish neighborhoods. Jerusalem has the largest non-Jewish, Palestinian population in Israel. Only a few thousand Palestinians hold Israeli citizenship. The majority hold merely a permanent residency document. Based on their ethno-national identity, the Jewish State and the municipality systematically discriminate against them in every sphere of urban reality, from allocation of financial resources through building permits and schools to garbage collection. The gaps between Jews and Palestinians in Jerusalem are well documented in NGO reports and not denied by the official authorities. Statistics show that Jerusalem is among the poorest cities in Israel. Yet, symbolically, it is on the top. More residents who are Jewish leave the city, between 6000-8000 annually, than choose to move to it. It is an unattractive place of living.

A Frontier City: Tension and Confrontation
Jerusalem is a tense place. So much so that seculars, many of whom reside in the Tel Aviv area, do not visit the city unless

they cannot avoid it. They report on feeling the city stress already twenty kilometers away from it. The city contains domestic Israeli conflicts between secular and orthodox Jews, rich and poor, left and right. Above all, it is the center of the Israeli-Palestinian conflict. Jerusalem, the national symbol for each side in the confrontation, is a frontier place.

My experience in London and Oxford taught me that Jerusalem is not a multicultural city; rather, it is a frontier city. Multicultural cities are composed of different linguistic-cultural minorities and of one dominant culture, whereas a frontier city is a city in which there is an ethnic-national confrontation between two communities. In Jerusalem, there is almost complete ecological segregation between Jews and Arabs, and the two sectors maintain separate public and private institutions and professional organizations. Day-to-day contact is largely utilitarian rather than social. The Jewish sector enjoys demographic, economic, and political supremacy and takes advantage of this reality to establish facts unilaterally in its favor.

Unlike a multicultural city, in which the minority feels disadvantaged because of its linguistic-cultural difference, in a frontier city the minority group does not see itself as inferior. This distinction derives from the fact that in a multicultural city the minorities view themselves as part of a common system that they share with the majority. Their dispute with the majority is about the legitimacy of their minority status, about the regime's policy toward them, and about the just division of resources. The members of the minority do not seek to break away from the system, but rather to integrate into it as a legitimate entity with equal rights. In a frontier city, by contrast, the minority seeks to delegitimize the rule of the majority, and to disengage in one way or another from that rule. Each of the communities in a frontier city sees itself to be of equal, if not higher, status than the other groups. Therefore, in a frontier city the principal question preoccupying the rivals is who the ruler is and who has the right to define the government's agenda. For the minority, the majority's policies, aimed at stability and continuity, are simply a means for perpetuating the majority's preeminence. In many cases, the government of the majority is unwilling to divide assets equitably, thus reinforcing the minority's demand for separation. Furthermore, in a frontier city, the demographic minority's case against the majority is not local, but rather represents one facet of the national confrontation. The national-ethnic gap prevails over the municipal boundaries defined by urban management, borders, and the supply of services, demographics, and territory. It takes on national significance and becomes part of the identities of each side. In contrast, the multicultural city does not embody a confrontation between national groups—at most, it reflects a social problem that characterizes the country itself within its boundaries. The multicultural city is heterogeneous, and there can be different coalitions between the ethnic groups that comprise it. These coalitions vary according to the issue at hand. In a frontier city, however, the polarization is deep and dichotomous, and the fissures that characterize it largely coincide with national fissures.

The 1967 War: A Turning Point

The conflict over Jerusalem is not a religious war. Whereas in pre-modern times the identity of the ruling power in Jerusalem was regarded as a sign indicating which religion God favors, in our time the focus is on national claims for self-determination and sovereignty. I lived this conflict before understanding it. As a child, I lived the divided city between Israel and Jordan, and as a boy I lived the 1967 war.

I had no idea on the morning of Monday, June 5, 1967, that a new era in history was dawning. There had been tension in the air for the previous three weeks. Everyone in Israel feared for the country's future, and I, fifteen years old at the time, was no different. I knew that Jerusalemites who had lived through the siege of 1948 had stocked up on food and fortified the entrances and windows of their homes with sandbags. But along the bus route through the city, I saw no sign that war was any closer than I had sensed the week before. By the time, however, that I arrived at the tall hill in West Jerusalem where my school stood, my classmates and I could see the war raging in the distance, on the city's eastern side. We heard muffled booms.

At around two in the afternoon, I decided to go home. I walked down to the Mt. Herzl military cemetery, on the main road, to catch my ride home. A bus was in flames. This was my first direct encounter with the war—a frightening though not a paralyzing sight. A passing driver offered to take me downtown. When I emerged from his car, I heard exploding shells and the crack of rifle fire. People told me not to walk up King George Street, which was in many places exposed to Jordanian snipers positioned on the Old City walls. Therefore, I made my way up silent side streets, holding my fears in check, intent on my goal of reaching my mother's office. When I got there, the few workers who remained in the building were huddled mutely in the basement, each sunk deep in his own fears. My mother was astonished to see me, but happy that I was unharmed. She did not say anything. I do not know how many memories of Auschwitz passed through her head. Did she doubt, at that moment, her fierce belief that Israel was a secure haven against another Holocaust? Did she fear she would lose her son, just as she had lost her home in the Second World War and her family at the death camp?

At 4:00 p.m., we decided that we'd be more comfortable at home, which was just a short walk to the south. When we got there and I went to my room, I found that the war had paid a visit—and that it had been a good thing that I had not been around when it did. My bed was covered with mortar shrapnel and stray bullets. I collected them, and they sit on my desk to this day. Home was clearly unsafe, so we headed for the communal bomb shelter in our building's basement, where we would have to live for the time being. There, too, my mother kept her feelings to herself. The loud sound of the war outside rendered us wordless and allowed us no rest. When, on Wednesday, I heard on my transistor radio that the Old City had been liberated, I liberated myself from the bomb shelter. A week later, the road to the Western Wall was open to Israelis. It was the Shavu'ot holiday. I walked confidently, one of a quarter-million Israelis, along the fenced-off path to the holy site. Two weeks later, the entire Old City was open. Tens of thousands of Israelis swept through it with an intense curiosity undergirded by an upwelling of victorious pride.

The nerve-wracking period before the war had proceeded at an agonizingly slow pace. Now life sped up. Every day brought some new experience. With my school friends, I skipped classes repeatedly to take in the Oriental *Shuk* and buy camels carved out of olive wood, fountain pens made in China, and Jordanian postcards, all items unknown in Israel until then. We were stupefied, trying to assimilate all the new sights. I personally experienced Jerusalem's opening to the east. It was incredibly intense for me. The transitions I had experienced were sudden and hard to digest—from a normal daily life to one of existential anxiety as the Arab countries placed Israel under siege. And from a sense that we were on the verge of a Holocaust, filling sandbags to protect our homes and preparing public parks to be used as mass graves, to an inspiring military victory—one of dimensions that Israel had not previously achieved (nor would it ever again). We had been living in a small country suffering from a severe recession; now we were citizens of a state that had acquired new territories several times larger than it previously possessed. A new regional power. Within a few months, the recession was over and the economy was thriving. Our sense of helplessness had now been replaced by arrogance and the intoxication of power. The western, Israeli side of Jerusalem had been the state's capital, but bereft of the major historical and religious sites of Jewish history and tradition, all of which had been on the Jordanian side. The new, reunited Jerusalem could now reestablish its roots in the Jewish past.

The war also transformed Jewish identity worldwide. Historically, it was Judaism that had combined religion and national identity. Ever since the June 1967 War, however, Jews imagine the State of Israel as the ultimate embodiment of their religious-national identity. In other words, the historically and theologically rich Judaism narrows to and identifies with a socio-political institution. Moreover, Jewish supremacy and Israeli state ethnocentrism are wrongly evaluated as Jewish. Neither demographically nor in its ruling methods can the city be considered Jewish.

Like most of my Israeli Jewish fellows, in 1967 and beyond, I viewed Jerusalem Palestinians as a collection of religious tribes different from mine. The Old City was perceived as an "open museum," merely the setting for a collection of Jewish archaeological and historical sites from the time of King David and the Second Temple. In this setting the Palestinians were passive, an echo of the past, a friendly, charming stranger. That passivity gave rise to the notion that they accepted Israeli sovereignty. The First Intifada in 1987, however, changed my mind. As a result, I moved my academic interest from modern Egypt to Israel-Palestine. In 1994, following the Oslo Accords, I started researching Jerusalem as a think-tank member preparing policy alternatives for Israeli-Palestinian final status talks. Later, it became one of my leading academic subjects. Meeting with Palestinian counterparts broadened my perspective on the city. In the 1990s, the myth of "united

Jerusalem, the eternal capital of Israel" dominated Israeli state agencies. The political leadership did not commission them to investigate the urban reality that clearly shows that the city is deeply divided between Israelis and Palestinians. Before and during the Camp David Summit in 2000, the Israeli delegation built its proposals on those policy papers.

Recommendations

I concluded from my studies that for the benefit of the two conflicting sides, sovereignty over the city should be divided along the principle that Arab neighborhoods belong to Palestine and Jewish ones to Israel. The Haram al-Sharif/Temple Mount will be under Palestinian sovereignty, and the Western Wall under Israeli sovereignty. Once national sovereignty is settled, the way is open to agree on mutual historical and religious attachment to the entire city. Urban studies show that cities with hard borders are underdeveloped and neglected. By contrast, free movement of people and goods, along with cultural exchange and interpersonal encounter, creates and maintains thriving cities. Therefore, Jerusalem must have open or very easy border crossings. Sure, security is necessary to maintain peace and a prosperous city, but hard borders built on mistrustfulness cannot bring peace. The "City of Justice," one of Jerusalem's titles in the Bible, is achievable by acknowledging that it belongs to all its residents equally. All must care about the place, and their everyday life perspective must be preferred over external interests and preserved.

14.

Jerusalem: The Cost of Jewish Israeli Dominance
Alice Rothchild

Evolving Awareness

As a Jew growing up in the United States, attending Hebrew school three times a week, services every Saturday morning, and the annual Passover Seders where we sang, "Next year in Jerusalem," I was grounded in an awareness of the centrality of that ancient city. I understood that Jerusalem's religious and historical significance was merged with a deep sense of holiness and yearning for Jews.

I also embraced my status as a member of a long-hated minority and a child of a politically progressive family. I claimed the heritage of Jews who had defended the disenfranchised, particularly in the labor, civil rights, and women's movements. I understood that to be Jewish not only meant to be an outsider and a survivor, but also to be chosen, not just in the Biblical sense, but also to be responsible for making the world a more just place. I loved Israel uncritically and saw the Israeli Defense Forces as my platonic idea of an army: moral, invincible, principled, and (most surprisingly) Jewish.

Although I grew increasingly skeptical of religious practice, during a 1964 family trip to Israel in my early teens, I recorded our visit to Jerusalem in a diary burning with keen observation loaded with negative assumptions about Arabs. Driving into the city, I wrote about Arabs "in their dirty headdresses" and "the ancient terraces built in the days of old," with no understanding of who exactly had been tending those gnarled and twisted grapevines and olive trees all those centuries. As I recorded in my diary:

> As we entered Jerusalem it seemed like we were going into a city less of the present than the past. We viewed the Jordanian border and spied on the Arab half of Jerusalem. Everywhere were the marks of war: bullet holes, barbed wire, sentry posts. Then we went to the tomb of King David. Here, each religion had added its piece, leaving a vivid picture of history in the buildings….

Forty years later, I returned as a student of history and as a political and human rights activist trying to make sense of the deeply fractured city. Over the following two decades, I immersed myself in examining the price of the triumphal Jewish narrative of "return" and "unification" and the consequences of a perceived eternal Jewish victimhood that gave birth to the belief that historic Palestine was "ours" at any cost. I grew to understand the blindness of otherwise decent, liberal-minded Jewish Israelis who were unable to see Palestinians as equally deserving human beings, brutally displaced in 1948 and again in 1967. My journey included interviewing, working with, and visiting many Palestinians living in East Jerusalem, the West Bank, and Gaza, detailing their experiences in essays, books, and a documentary film.

I placed my perceptions of Jerusalem in the context of my developing understanding of the history of the founding of the state, which contradicted many of the myths I was exposed to in Hebrew school and at home. The work of the Zionist movement to establish an exclusive Jewish state in historic Palestine became a reality through a confluence of factors. These included European anti-Semitism, the Christian Zionism of colonial British leaders, the appalling consequences of the Nazi Holocaust, and the UN's attempts to address the desperate needs of postwar European Jewish refugees who were not welcomed in other countries. The underlying racism that allowed European Jewish trauma, aspirations, and history to be privileged at the expense of the indigenous Palestinian population was rarely acknowledged, or else justified in the name of Jewish survival.

At the same time, I came to realize, much like societies colonized in other parts of the world, that the people who were living in historic Palestine (Muslims, Christians, and a small number of Jews) could not be expected to relinquish peacefully the land and homes they had lived in for centuries. Zionism had been sold to me as a redemptive Jewish liberation movement building a new and just society for a battered people in their ancestral lands. Meanwhile, religious Jews yearned for the Messiah, and Christian Zionists awaited the Rapture; both belief systems required Jews to "return" to Zion, albeit for very opposite reasons. In the maelstrom of these political forces, Palestinians (Muslims and Christians) were rendered virtually invisible, often defined as "implacable enemies" or "terrorists." This is the context in which I came to understand Jerusalem.

Exploring the city, I found it to be a montage of stunning contrasts: new and old, West and East, Jewish, Christian, and Muslim, where the layers of history were clearly apparent, every occupier making claim, building homes, temples, churches, mosques, often on top of each other. The extraordinary richness, beauty, and complexity of the place led me to be haunted by three questions: Why do Jewish Israeli claims take precedence over everyone else who has inhabited the city? Why do the needs and demands of Jews who have emigrated from Warsaw, Poland, or Brooklyn, New York, negate the claims of families who have actually lived in the city for centuries? What is the price of these policies for Jews as well as Palestinians?

Living Conditions

In 2011, I met Abu Hassan in front of the Jerusalem Hotel for a walking/bus tour of the city. He explained that since 1967 when Israeli forces captured East Jerusalem, Palestinians from East Jerusalem have been, and still are, *residents* of the city, not *citizens* of Israel. After the war, they refused to accept Israeli citizenship because that would have negated their political rights to the city they once fully inhabited. For Palestinians in East Jerusalem to retain their residency IDs, they had to prove repeatedly that they lived within the Jerusalem borders. In 2005 the Israeli government stopped all residency applications. This caused a host of problems. If an East Jerusalemite man married a West Bank woman, she could not legally live with him, and if he moved to the West Bank, he would not be allowed to return to East Jerusalem. Hundreds of Palestinian families had "weekend relationships" with each partner retaining residency in their place of origin, shuttling themselves and their growing families back and forth, or living "illegally" in Jerusalem without access to services and with constant fear of deportation. East Jerusalem Palestinians who traveled abroad for work or education were at risk for losing their IDs due to often obscure and changing regulations and a strangling bureaucracy.

Abu Hassan's family had lived in Jerusalem for generations; an uncle lived in the neighborhood of Abu Dis. In 1967, the Israeli government declared his section of the community part of the West Bank. He lost his East Jerusalem ID and was unable to return to the city.

Since the Israeli government established East Jerusalem in 1967 as part of a "unified city," 40 percent of the land has been confiscated as military zone or green space that was then developed for Jewish settlements. The erasure of the Palestinian presence continued with the building of a bridge and a tram so that Jewish settlers could avoid traveling through Palestinian areas and prevent contact with the Palestinian population.

Abu Hassan pointed out the settlement of Pisgat Ze'ev, established in the 1980s and now one of the biggest colonies in East Jerusalem with 34,000 Jewish settlers, built on land from the Palestinian villages of Shu'fat and Beit Hanina. The separation wall near Pisgat Ze'ev surrounded Palestinian villages and the Shu'fat refugee camp; 60,000 refugees had one entrance/exit; they needed to have an East Jerusalem ID to pass. In this bizarre world, 20 percent of the inhabitants within this curve of the wall had West Bank IDs and were married to East Jerusalemites; they had two options: stay on the camp side of the wall or move to the West Bank.

East Jerusalemites paid the same taxes as those in the West but received 20 percent of the public services. The Jewish Quarter of the Old City was clean and well-kept as opposed to the grime, garbage, and disrepair of the Arab sector. Abu Hassan pointed out the roof tops: Jewish houses had white water towers for hot water; Palestinian houses had the white towers, but also black towers because their water supply was not reliable and additional water storage was collected when available. In addition, they paid five times as much for this precious commodity. East Jerusalemites were similarly disadvantaged when it came to electricity; permits to expand or build homes were (and continue to be) virtually impossible to obtain.

We drove into the expanding Jewish settlement of Pisgat Ze'ev, rows of neat, well-groomed apartments, a mall and good transportation, modern local services, a playground and swimming pool. By contrast, nearby Palestinians were faced with a severe shortage of schools. For the last two years, 150 Palestinian children had been unable to find schooling. The catch-22 was that when the child turned 16 and applied for an East Jerusalem residency ID, the parents had to prove that the child attended school within the Jerusalem borders by providing a yearly diploma and documentation that both parents were from East Jerusalem.

Abu Hassan explained that he had married a German woman. He struggled for twelve years to get her a residency ID; meanwhile, she was not allowed to leave the country or work and thus had no health insurance. After five years, the residency laws changed; he had to start the process all over again. The lawyer's fees amounted to $15,000, but now he was assured his four children would be able to get their IDs. Jews were encouraged by Israel to buy apartments, often at one-third the market value, with reduced tax collection.

On the right we passed a cascade of grey houses, the Shu'fat Refugee Camp, established in 1967 when families who had lived in Jerusalem for generations were removed by the Israeli military from the area adjacent to the Western Wall. 17,000 people crowded into one square kilometer. They started living in tents provided by UNRWA (United Nations Relief and Works Agency, responsible for Palestinian refugees), moved into concrete houses, and were now expanding vertically. The camp was surrounded by high concrete walls, but from the upper stories of the apartments, refugees could see the well-maintained Jewish settlements, the confiscated land, the green lawns, and swimming pools. Many of the citizens of Pisgat Ze'ev were from Brooklyn, Kahanists famous for their violent racism. Abu Hassan reported that there was now a Jewish Defense League that waited for Palestinian youth at the mall to attack them, unrestrained by police.

We arrived at the Sheikh Jarrah neighborhood and stood in front of the house of the evicted al-Ghawi family, whom I had met the previous year living in a tent outside their property. In 2009, 800 soldiers and police evicted 37 members of this family from their homes. We watched a man with a large black hat and long black coat rush into their apartment that was topped by a gigantic menorah. The Palestinian family still received the water and electricity bills as they refused to change the registration.

We visited an elderly Palestinian woman who had been evicted from her home where she had lived for many decades with her family, extending the one-story building to accommodate her children and grandchildren. During a recent eviction, Jewish settlers were moved into the front portion of her house, now draped with a large Israeli flag and adorned with Stars of David painted around the front window. This woman was forced to live in the back portion with her son and grandchildren. Their case was in the Israeli courts, where there was little chance they would be treated favorably. At any time, this family, like others in the neighborhood, could be evicted forcibly and put out on the street with their meager possessions.

Demolitions

Suddenly, a friend of Abu Hassan arrived and showed him a photo on his phone. A demolition was underway. Abu Hassan explained that the former house of the Grand Mufti of Jerusalem, which became a hotel and then a center for the Shin Bet (Israel's internal security agency), was being demolished to build 500 homes for Jewish settlers. We hustled back into the bus and drove to the area that was crowded with cars and press. The large, yellow Volvo bulldozers could be seen smashing at the walls, creating clouds of debris. A crowd of reporters, cameramen, and angry protesters gathered. An older woman with a purple hijab spoke, gesturing animatedly to a white-haired man, Elisha Peleg, a member of the City Council. The general tone of the crowd was one of frustration and rage at yet another land grab in East Jerusalem, another violation of international law, another nail in the coffin of a Palestinian state.

Peleg argued that this demolition was legal, citing a variety of administrative procedures. "We have a right to have Jewish families in this unified city. I am very proud of what we are doing." He said Arabs could easily get permits to build in West Jerusalem (false), and then accused the protesters of racism. He angrily questioned if any Arabs had papers to prove they were evicted from properties in Jerusalem, had gone through proper channels, and so forth. This provoked hostile responses from several Arab men who clearly had personal experiences with dispossession and familiarity with Israel's antagonistic permit application and judicial systems. People started chanting, "Shame! Shame!" I noticed heavily armed security guards in civilian clothes moving closer. At one point a woman yelled, "You are delusional!" Peleg looked at her and said, "What is this, delusional?"

Abu Hassan explained that his conflict was not with Jews; in fact, his family took care of an Iraqi Jewish woman in their own home for years. His conflict was with Zionists who wanted to push Palestinians off the land they had called their own for generations. East Jerusalem was one of the battlegrounds, and the Palestinians were losing in the face of byzantine administrative rules, outright lying, brutal violence, a society that had grown increasingly racist and supportive of rightwing ideologies, and an international community that had completely abdicated its responsibilities.

It was a sobering and emotional experience for me to see the violations of international law and the Judaization of East Jerusalem happening in real time, surrounded by the people who were watching the Israeli government irreversibly colonize their land which the international community recognized as occupied territory.

Manipulating Demography

These demolitions and expulsions occur within a context. I found that in the late 1990s and early 2000s, the Israeli government produced a multi-volume Master Plan, with thousands of pages devoted to Jerusalem. The goal was to control Palestinian demographics and to increase the Jewish presence. Through a combination of Judaization and ethnic cleansing, the intention was to decrease the Palestinian population from 35 percent to 12 percent. With almost scientific precision, this is what has been unfolding over the past two decades.

Israel planned to expand the boundaries of Greater Jerusalem to include Jewish settlement blocks, surrounding them with the imposing separation wall snaking deep into the West Bank and ghettoizing the local Palestinians. Twenty-two villages with 225,300 people who had once been part of Jerusalem would then be outside of the Holy City. Within the Old City, the changes started with the destruction of the neighborhood along the Wailing Wall and then the allotment of millions of shekels to Judaize the area, ultimately displacing the residents of Silwan, now officially the "City of David," moving in Jewish families, house by house. The final step was the establishment of a highly politicized and severely criticized archeological excavation in the City of David, designed to prove exclusively Jewish claims to a city that had been occupied innumerable times over thousands of years, displacing 1,500 Palestinians to make space for a parking lot for tourist buses. The Israelis planned to continue a similar process in the neighborhoods of Shu'fat and Sheikh Jarrah and to link them all together with a light rail that ends at the Damascus Gate, gradually eliminating the presence of Palestinians. I learned of multiple well-funded new projects: museums, hotels, tunnels under the ancient walls, car parks, tourist overviews, and new synagogues, including one to be built next to the wall of the Old City.

The Future

None of this happens by accident; the future of Jerusalem will clearly be built by the steady march of Israeli bulldozers, the pounding of construction projects, and the whine of tear gas and bullets. Whenever I hear of efforts by Jewish extremists to pray at Haram al-Sharif/Temple Mount in the shadows of the Al-Aqsa Mosque and Dome of the Rock, or to construct a Jewish temple on the site, I am filled with grief. When I hear of Israeli government plans to build on top of a Muslim cemetery or extend the Jerusalem Walls National Park to include the Mount of Olives, violating properties privately owned by Palestinians and by Franciscan, Armenian, and Greek Orthodox churches, I am filled with anger. When another family in Sheikh Jarrah is thrown into the street, another Palestinian boy is shot by a soldier or a settler, another archeological site is developed by Elad, the tourist and archeology settler organization, to promote a nationalistic ideological agenda, I can only shake my head in despair. When thousands of men in kippahs, wrapped in blue and white Israeli flags, march defiantly in the annual Jerusalem Day parade chanting "Death to Arabs," or a Palestinian family "self-demolishes" their home to avoid paying huge fines, I feel ashamed to be a Jew. Jerusalem is a vivid example of the failure of Zionism, the cost of a supremacist Jewish ideology that demonizes Muslims and Christians and people identified as Arab and allows a thuggish rightwing element of the population to flower. In Jerusalem, I feel the loss of the prophetic traditions that have been central to Judaism. I see the demise of decency and tolerance in an historic city that could have been shared amongst three Abrahamic faiths and might have been an example for the rest of the world. Instead, this city with so much potential, has been lost to a righteous, racist settler colonial state.

15.
My Transformative Journey
Aleen Bayard

A Brief History of My Jewrusalem

Prior to the fall of 2021, when my husband and I joined a "dual narrative" tour in Israel, Jerusalem didn't mean much to me. That is not a cavalier or disrespectful statement. Jerusalem held the same significance as other world capitals on my bucket list such as Paris, London, or Buenos Aires. Even though I was raised and identified as being Jewish for most of my life, Jerusalem was an agnostic landmark, not a spiritual destination.

In that vein, I had previously visited Jerusalem, twice, as a tourist. In the first instance, I was nine years old, carted to Europe and the Middle East with my younger sister and brother by our parents who relocated us from our Chicago apartment to a VW camper to travel abroad, with our final destination being Israel. I had absolutely no comprehension of the political and social context that was paramount during the time of our family trip in 1968. An older, more aware and sophisticated me would have appreciated the fact that our three-week visit transpired less than a year after the Six-Day War. The fact that an Israeli soldier toting a very large rifle accompanied us as we drove from Jerusalem south to Masada was thrilling for my siblings and me. My parents understood his presence was not coincidental or random, as was that of many of the hitchhikers we picked up during our drive through the desert, but rather he was there as a deterrent to protect a young American family on that summer afternoon.

My second visit was equally and woefully politically tone deaf. This trip was planned to celebrate my husband's milestone birthday and was marked by a wrenching trip to Yad Vashem, a fascinating tour of the Weizmann Institute, and a six-minute dash into a lovely gift shop along the Mamilla Mall to pick up trinkets for my BFFs at home. During those two weeks, I do not recall seeing or speaking to a single Palestinian. If I had, I would have mistakenly identified such a person as an Arab as I grouped all Arabic speakers into a single demographic. Despite a pedigreed education and self-identification as a "global citizen," I was illiterate in the case of the Middle East. There were Arabs and Jews. I did not make the distinction between Arabs and Muslims, nor did I understand that there are Palestinian Muslims *and* Palestinian Christians. As I walked the streets of Jerusalem's Old City during that visit, I entirely missed the fact that the Holy Sepulchre, Christianity's most holy site, was mere steps from the Wailing Wall.

But, as the saying goes, the third time is the charm. And so, it was.

My third visit to Jerusalem in 2021 was simply transformative. I was in Jerusalem on the coattails of a Combatants for Peace expedition arranged by Medji Tours. This particular tour was unlike any I have been on. For rather than the customary visits to ancient ruins, world-class museums, and mindless sightseeing, we toured refugee camps, witnessed what many (myself included) viewed as evidence of apartheid, and heard the stories of Israelis and Palestinians grappling with fear, inequity, and violence. The program was masterfully designed by and partially chaperoned by Aziz Abu Sarah, one of two founders of Mejdi Tours, which promotes the idea of a "more peaceful and interconnected world through travel" (https://www.mejditours.com/home-mejdi/). Mr. Abu

Sarah has personally experienced many of the disparities faced by Palestinians living in and around Jerusalem, a reality we fellow travelers appreciated when we were bussed from our hotel, a block from the Damascus Gate, to eat dinner at Mr. Abu Sarah's childhood home, located in Area B, a neighborhood chiefly inhabited by Palestinians, but under Israeli security control. For Palestinians, the 20-minute drive is congested by a menacing type of traffic: cars are halted by poking machine guns, not careless fender-benders. His own parents and siblings need a permit and must go through a checkpoint to travel from their living room to enter Jerusalem's center. The Israeli guard at the checkpoint that evening merely waved *us* through without looking up from his newspaper. These instances of dualism constituted the souvenirs I collected as a researcher and a human being.

As the dual narrative tour unfolded, and I saw Jerusalem through the eyes of Israelis *and* Palestinians, I came to appreciate Jerusalem as a visceral paradox of hope and hopelessness, of sacred prayer and naked hostility, of unity and division. Jerusalem revealed the best and most incomprehensible aspects of our human family. She also was the patient midwife as I birthed the answers to my research questions.

Pathways to Reconciliation

My newfound and hard-won appreciation for Jerusalem was earned as a byproduct of my dissertation research, which focused on reconciliation within the context of peacebuilding. My research explored the attitudes and experiences of individual peacebuilders who are joining with former adversaries to create the conditions of positive peace in regions plagued by generational conflict.

Within the broad field of peacebuilding scholarship, the scales are decidedly tipped to study phenomena around conflict resolution, transitional justice, and third-party interventions.

While these areas represent legitimate efforts to negotiate treaties and monitor compliance between state actors, history has shown the Sisyphean nature of these approaches in terms of implementation and securing sustainable peace. Therefore, I chose to study individuals who are currently acting in some capacity of building positive peace and are doing so in many cases in partnership or cooperation with sworn enemies. I wanted to understand how individual peacebuilders participating in these efforts are able to reconcile with former enemies to build a new future. I was drawn to investigate an apparent vacuum: What is happening on the ground once the peace treaties are signed and reparations are made? How do ordinary people come to terms with past injustices to create a new future? In Jerusalem, the question is particularly challenging as the injustices continue in both subtle and menacing ways through Israel's occupation of contested territorial lands.

Spoken by an American Jew, the prior sentence is somewhat heretical. We don't hear about Israel as an occupier. We hear about suicide bombers and rocket attacks and other acts of terrorism committed on behalf of or directly by Palestinians. It is a one-sided narrative, and one that I consumed without question. The storyline is so perfected and so pervasive, it had become invisible to me. Palestinians were the bad guys, and Israelis, the good ones.

This worldview was prevalent during my *second* visit to Jerusalem, and it manifested in the following scenario.

My husband and I had just left the Jaffa Gate and were headed toward the Citadel to explore the archeological remains of King David's palace. Our (Israeli) tour guide took the opportunity to point out the rooftops and streetscape of an adjacent neighborhood that was clearly in decline. He pointed out the differences between the dirty streets strewn with garbage and adorned by graffiti and the much tidier and well-kept blocks we walked through. The message was anything but subtle. In fact, he said, "The Arabs don't take care of their own neighborhoods." This juxtaposition of insinuated neglect by one population and the superiority of another occurred frequently as we toured the country. I drank the Kool-Aid without knowing a beverage was being served. The photo below illustrates the point made by the tour guide regarding the poor condition of Palestinian neighborhoods. What he failed to mention are the many Israeli policies crippling prosperity (and pride) in these very same areas.

Which made the third and most recent visit to Jerusalem so transformative. It was in this instance, accompanied by both Israeli and Palestinian tour guides, I at once discovered my own myopias and was able to correct my vision. I answered my own research question as I reconciled the paradox that peace and violence co-exist and that peacebuilders can view the other as a threat and still join together to foster conditions of coexistence.

Symbols of occupation

The core of the conflict between Israelis and Palestinians is rooted in and fueled by Israel's policies and its occupation of the West Bank. One need look no further than the use of the term "occupation" to understand why Jerusalem is so meaningful to anyone concerned with achieving peace in the Holy Land. It is in Jerusalem, quite prevalently in the Old City, that this occupation seeps and crawls so cunningly.

Two personal anecdotes illuminate this phenomenon.

Our group was walking through the Old City, actually on the very pathway taken by Jesus as he carried the cross on his shoulders. The Old City is divided, separated, organized, or in some fashion described as having quarters populated by Muslims, Jews, Armenians, and Christians. On the surface, this clustering can be viewed as quaint and sensible. I saw it as such (akin to similar wanderings through Chinatown in San Francisco and Greektown in Chicago). In these cases, different ethnicities and cultures are celebrated. At one point, our guide asked us to look up and asked us, "What do you see?", a seemingly benign question. I saw a row of Israeli flags perched from windows on what was presumably a second or third floor as captured in the photo on the next page.

Our guide proceeded to explain that these flags were placed by Israeli settlers who had taken over occupancy of several apartments previously inhabited by Palestinians. Their "residency" was in direct conflict with the policies within the Old City, and the flags were a constant reminder of their presence. For many Palestinians, the Israeli flag is a symbol of violence, harassment, and sometimes, death.

"I have always feared the Israeli flag. I see the flag, and I think of the daily invasions. Of the soldiers coming into my house. Of my friends who were shot, wrongfully," chillingly noted a subject of my research who works with the Holy Land Trust, https://www.holylandtrust.org/, which fosters peace, justice, healing, and transformation.

These flags are as powerful as bullets to the psyche of the Palestinian who stops to buy spices and dates or have a haircut or a cup of mint tea. These flags have become an agonizing reminder of what Jerusalem means to me. It is a place where faith and blasphemy exist within a few feet of each other.

A second example of this type of silent violence and oppressive threat occurred on the terrace below the steps leading to Al-Aqsa, one of the most sacred holy sites in the

Muslim world. Our group had spent an hour engaging with the two dozen women and their children who were seemingly picnicking outside the mosque. Bread, cheese, smiles, and a few words of Arabic were exchanged to the delight of all parties. My husband taught a group of young boys how to choreograph a secret handshake routine as they high-fived, fist-bumped, and twirled on the 3,000-year-old stones. Their enthusiastic thumbs-up was the proverbial cherry on top of a truly magical encounter.

Everyone was beaming, and I felt a sense of calm and serenity moving so freely among this now intimate group. In 2015, on my second visit to Jerusalem, tourists were forbidden from visiting Al-Aqsa due to recent violence. It was nothing short of miraculous that we were able to freely wander around the mosque. Even our Israeli guide noted how remarkable it was for her to be welcomed by the group of pilgrims.

We said goodbye and walked down the flight of stairs to regroup before continuing our tour. At that moment, several men approached the bottom of the steps and stood motionless, looking up at the worshipers outside the mosque. These men were clearly Jewish. I identified them easily with their black hats, worn prayer books, and strings of tallis hanging below their white shirts. I was curious as to their presence. It was provocative. Our guide explained the men were settlers who frequently come to this place to intimidate the people going into the mosque. Without uttering a word, they were intrusive, as evidenced by the fact that the children who had been giggling and offering us pieces of sweet bread and candy were now hiding behind their mothers' long dresses, eyes downcast, backing away.

They carried no visible weapons, fired no bullets, and did not approach a single person. And yet, their mere presence extinguished the sparks of friendship and joy we had ignited just moments before.

Holes in our History Books

Jerusalem is also the site of the Nakba, an event that is held as a searing a memory in the minds of present-day Palestinians. In 30 years of higher education in the U.S., I had never heard this term or had any exposure to the history of the Palestinian people. My context was entirely formed by passionate rabbis and well-meaning Sunday school teachers in Reform synagogues who taught me about the Maccabees, the Second Temple, Passover, and the Holocaust. I was proud to be Jewish. I was loyal to Israel. While I wasn't entirely sure what a Zionist was, I probably would have answered "yes" if asked. In all those weekend mornings learning our history and attending sermons, no one ever mentioned the plight of the Palestinians. I knew the Jews fled Europe after the Second World War. What was MIA from both secular and non-secular references was mention of the seminal event in the history of the other heirs to the Holy Land. The Nakba, translated as the Catastrophe, continues to haunt thousands of families who still hold hope of returning.

On our dual narrative tour, we learned the significance of painted keys in the murals adorning many walls around Jerusalem. These keys represent defiance, will, and the hope of returning…home.

Reflections

What Jerusalem means to me has evolved over the half century I have travelled there. My nine-year-old self took no notice of the differences between one Israeli city and the next. I recognized some part of myself in Tel Aviv, Haifa, and Jerusalem. It was like being in temple during the High Holidays—all the time. Everybody and everything was Jewish. Jerusalem solidified my identity and strengthened my heritage.

Image of key on wall in refugee camp on the outskirts of Jerusalem

My second visit as an adult was colored by the right-wing views of our guide. Being entirely ill-equipped and uneducated, I had no rebukes or rebuttals or even challenges to his presentation. Jerusalem was a photo opportunity to capture the many historical references to injustices and anti-Semitism.

Today, I celebrate Jerusalem as a mecca of transformation. In this place, I met the heroes and heroines on the front lines of peacebuilding. Israelis who wait for hours at a checkpoint to accompany a Palestinian mother and her sick daughter to a hospital for cancer treatment, providing much-needed transportation and translation services to ease what is already a challenging and frightening experience. Palestinians who, under the threat of being termed "normalizers" and facing dangerous acts of retribution, partner with Israelis to provide access to clean water and safe passage for Bedouin farmers.

Tragic events continue to plague this wondrous city. Headlines attest to the seemingly unsatiable appetite for revenge and violence. Those unspeakable acts will always and forever be in the shadow of the fervent prayers of the faithful. Jerusalem is a holy place for all in the Holy Land.

16.

My Story: Jerusalem as Source of Lifelong Inspiration and Career Path
Martin J. Raffel

Growing up in a traditional Jewish home, I perfunctorily recited the line at the end of our Passover Seders, "Next Year in Jerusalem." When attending services in my synagogue on the Sabbath and Jewish holidays, the rest of the congregation and I chanted our prayers facing Jerusalem. Little did I know that this unique city, depicted in a famous medieval map as the center of the world, would come to play a pivotal role in the shaping of my identity and professional life for some five and a half decades.

Jerusalem: Stage One, 1968-69
My first direct encounter with the Holy City came in October 1968 when I began a junior year abroad at the American College in Jerusalem, its first year in operation. While I was raised to have a strong Jewish identity, and attended a Harrisburg, Pennsylvania, Jewish day school through eighth grade, our home was not particularly Israel-oriented. I never participated in a Zionist organization or youth group. Thus, the idea of spending an extended length of time in Israel was not in the forefront of my mind. That said, my mother's intrepid younger sister and longtime educator, Elkie Koplovitz, traveled to Israel in the summer of 1967, well before it became commonplace to do so. Her stories of Jerusalem, especially the

thrill of standing next to the Western Wall, no doubt, seeped into my consciousness.

How did the decision to study in Israel come about? The first two years of my college education were spent at Franklin & Marshall in Lancaster, Pennsylvania. In those times, F&M was an all-boys institution; it would transition to co-ed in my senior year. While, on the one hand, the academics were first rate (I was thinking about law school and a career in some public interest field)—on the other hand, the all-male social environment was unpleasant. Consequently, I merely latched on to an overseas program that would take me out of that environment for a year. Unlike today, when there are numerous overseas study options, Israel was one of a small number of such programs in the late 1960s. Also, it seemed to be the only option that offered a full academic year abroad, not only one semester.

My early experience in Jerusalem must be understood in the context of the American scene I left behind in October 1968. It is hard to imagine a more tumultuous time, particularly on college campuses. The anti-Vietnam War movement was in full swing. The assassination of Martin Luther King, Jr. set the country ablaze, both literally and figuratively. Robert Kennedy's assassination dashed the hopes of many young people who believed that he could win the presidency and end the war. The Democratic Convention in the summer of 1968 in Chicago was a fiasco, which probably led to Hubert Humphrey's defeat by Richard Nixon several months later. There were heightened tensions in the country, even within families. My father, a decorated World War II veteran, had a hard time accepting my opposition to the war and to service in the U.S. military. Many of my peers and I were deeply resentful that our government was sending us off to kill and be killed in a conflict with which we fundamentally disagreed.

The atmosphere in Israel, just over a year after the 1967 Six-Day War, was virtually the opposite. The young generation of Israelis loved their country, felt they had won a just war of self-defense, and had great confidence in their government. Israelis exulted in the reunification of Jerusalem, which had been divided—with Jews denied access to their holy places—since their 1948 War of Independence.

I loved spending time late at night at the Western Wall in the Old City when it was quiet and free of large crowds, especially visitors who saw it as just another tourist attraction. I sat next to the huge Herodian stones, felt the breeze on my face, and pretended to hear the voices of my ancestors from centuries, even millennia, ago. The Jewish people's connection with this land, I internalized, was deep and eternal. And, for me, it quickly became a personal connection.

Of course, I readily understood that Jerusalem does not belong to the Jewish people alone. Indeed, the first glimpse of the Dome of the Rock Mosque, holy to Muslims, nearly took my breath away. I eagerly absorbed the rich multi-cultural, interfaith dimensions of the city. Another one of my favorite things to do was to place myself at a location in the Old City where I could hear, as though a symphony, Jews praying at the Western Wall, the Muslim call to prayer from the Al Aqsa Mosque, and the bells of the Church of the Holy Sepulchre. Religious passions in Jerusalem are palpable. I recognized that this convergence of the Abrahamic faiths' holy sites within such a small geographic space gives Jerusalem's Old City its spiritual power and, unfortunately, also its danger and tragedy.

During that year, I befriended a fellow student who lived in the Armenian Quarter of the Old City. I visited many times there, attending family celebrations and, more importantly for him and for me, learning about the Armenian genocide at the hands of the Turks in 1915-16. During Orthodox Easter in 1969, he invited me to attend the Holy Fire ceremony at the

Church of the Holy Sepulchre as an "honorary" member of the Armenian community. The ceremony, which celebrates Jesus's resurrection, involves Jerusalem's Greek Orthodox patriarch entering the tomb where Christians believe Jesus was buried and emerging shortly thereafter, seemingly as if by miracle, with a lit candle. The flame from this one candle is then spread around to hundreds of people inside the church with their own candles until the entire sanctuary is aglow. I was deeply moved by the ceremony and by my friend's generosity in allowing me to share in this event with his community. Many Christian pilgrims wait their whole lives for the chance to participate in this ceremony. I could not know at the time that, one day, I would have the chance to encourage the organized Jewish community to officially recognize the Armenian genocide. It was an objective I failed to accomplish, but not for lack of trying.

As my studies at the American College neared an end, I was able to observe the Yom Hazikaron (Remembrance Day) ceremony, which honors Israel's fallen soldiers, at the military cemetery on Mt. Herzl. Then Prime Minister Golda Meir was keynote speaker. I wrote to my parents afterwards: "Hundreds of mothers sat in rows by their sons' graves. At the end [of the ceremony], Hatikvah (Israel's national anthem) was played with their sobbing in the background, the City of Jerusalem off in the distance. At that moment, I could have been convinced to live in Israel by just about anybody."

Another takeaway from that year in Jerusalem was an understanding that there were no angels and devils in the Israeli-Palestinian conflict. As one of my professors observed, "It isn't a conflict between right and wrong, but rather between right and right." If Jews were entitled to national self-determination, I reasoned early on, why not also the Palestinians? Though surrounded by the euphoria of Jerusalem's reunification, I even envisioned sharing sovereignty in Jerusalem—only if

Israel's security was assured, and the city would never again be divided.

Jerusalem: Stage Two, 1969-78

Upon returning to F&M for senior year, my study focus shifted. I started taking classes in Middle East issues, especially the Israel-Arab conflict. The year after graduation I came back to Israel, spent about six months on several kibbutzim, and attended intensive Hebrew classes at an Ulpan (a Hebrew language school for adults) to improve my grasp of the language. The original idea of becoming an American civil rights / civil liberties lawyer ebbed. I began to ask how I would integrate a connection to Israel into my life. I considered law school in Israel. In the end, I decided to attend law school at American University (AU) in Washington, DC.

My law school experience at AU was positive. Yet, I couldn't fully focus on anything except Israel. So, at the end of the first year, I returned to Jerusalem, enrolled at the Hebrew University School of Law, and resolved to use my degree to infuse the Israeli legal system with an American-style public interest sensibility. Maybe this could be achieved, I thought, by founding an organization patterned after the American Civil Liberties Union. My intention was to make Aliyah and become an Israeli citizen under the Law of Return, which grants automatic citizenship to Jews.

Studying law in the Hebrew language—understanding the lectures and reading lengthy court decisions—was challenging. Many of my American family members and friends would ask me whether classes were in Hebrew or English. I smiled and said, "You know, it is Israel, after all, and the language of the country is Hebrew." They were impressed.

As we were about to enter our second year of law school, an earthquake shook Israel—the 1973 Yom Kippur War. I was in the U.S. when war broke out, but quickly returned to a somber Jerusalem. We began to learn of fallen classmates who would not be returning to their studies. A close friend was doing his reserve duty at the Suez Canal when the Egyptian army stormed Israeli fortifications. He did return to school and was an excellent student. Yet, emotionally, he was never the same. There weren't many young Israeli men in Jerusalem at that time; they all remained in uniform. It was awkward riding public transportation. The buses were full of women, children, and old men who all stared as I boarded. They did not comprehend why I wasn't serving at the front. While law school was suspended indefinitely, I volunteered to teach a gym class at an elementary school in French Hill, a Jerusalem neighborhood built after 1967. I replaced the regular teacher, who had to remain in the army for months after the war was over. It gave me a sense of satisfaction knowing I was helping on the home front. Also, using the unexpected free time, which lasted until school finally reopened in early 1974, I started studying Arabic at a language school in the Old City.

Life as a student in Jerusalem settled in. Besides legal studies, I played rugby for the first time in my life and represented the Hebrew University against teams from other parts of Israel. I came away from the experience with new friends and a very painful broken nose.

In Israel, as in Britain, there is a requirement to clerk with either a judge or a senior attorney prior to taking the bar exam. I spent two years clerking: the first at the State Attorney's office of Israel's Ministry of Justice and the second in Jerusalem's District Attorney's office. In the second year, I got to appear on my own in misdemeanor cases before Jerusalem's Magistrates Court. One of the teachers at the Jewish day school I attended once complained to my despairing parents that, in his opinion, I would never be able to master even basic Hebrew. So much for that prediction!

At the end of my two years clerking, I passed the bar exam. As a full-fledged lawyer, I got a job in the Legal Aid division of the Ministry of Justice and spent a little less than a year representing indigent clients in the Magistrates, Rabbinical, and Labor Courts. By then, I was driving to work, a route that took me around the Old City's walls that were built by the Turkish Sultan Suleiman in 1535. On those trips, I often thought of my grandparents, who immigrated to the United States from Lithuania and Belarus in the late nineteenth and early twentieth centuries. Like them, I believed I was beginning a new story line for my family that would affect the lives of future generations.

Jerusalem: Stage Three, 1978-Present
In March 1978, I returned to the U.S. for what I expected and hoped would be an interval of several years. The plan was to return and resume my professional legal trajectory in Jerusalem. After spending one year in a law firm in my hometown and becoming a member of the Pennsylvania Bar, I decided to pursue work in the Jewish community relations field. In the fall of 1979, I became assistant director of the American Jewish Committee in Philadelphia. My work involved reaching out to non-Jewish coalition partners to address a wide range of local, state, and national issues. Israel was only part of the agency's agenda. In 1983, I became director of the American Jewish Congress' Philadelphia office, and our focus was on the First Amendment and church-state issues.

By then I was married and had started thinking about a family, and the plan to return to Israel slowly started to recede. Not completely. My wife, Maris Chavenson, who had little or no background on Israel and had never been there, bravely offered to try living there if I wanted to return. By the time I received an offer of an interesting professional opportunity in Jerusalem that I would have taken had it come earlier, our children already were in elementary school. I wasn't prepared to dislocate them at that sensitive age for the sake of fulfilling my Zionist dream.

During my tenure at the American Jewish Congress, my wife and I traveled to what is now the Former Soviet Union (FSU) in 1984 for the purpose of clandestinely meeting with Refuseniks. These were Jews whose requests for visas to immigrate to Israel had been refused by the Soviet bureaucracy and who then suffered harassment, loss of jobs, and in some cases (e.g., Anatoly [Natan] Sharansky) even imprisonment. We visited three cities: Moscow, St. Petersburg (then Leningrad), and Vilnius. Many of my ancestors lived near Vilnius before coming to the United States in the latter part of the nineteenth century.

For me, the highlight of the FSU experience came in Moscow when I was asked to address, in Hebrew, some twenty young Russian Jews who were teaching the language to children in the city, an activity then forbidden under Soviet law. We met in an apartment building basement behind a locked door. As I started to speak, there was a loud banging on the door. These brave Hebrew teachers said, "Don't worry. Go ahead. It's just the police. They try to disrupt our activities all the time." I somewhat nervously proceeded to share—admittedly with tears in my eyes—what the American Jewish community was doing on their behalf. But most of my talk, using the Hebrew I had acquired in Israel, was spent describing the beauty of Jerusalem, the city they so yearned to see and possibly live in one day.

While work at the two AJCs was interesting, what I really wanted was a position that would enable me to deal with Israel-related issues fulltime. That opportunity came in 1987 when I was named Israel Director of the Jewish Council for Public Affairs (JCPA). This became a career job. I retired from the JCPA in 2014.

The JCPA is an umbrella body of national Jewish groups, including the American Jewish Committee, the Anti-Defamation League, B'nai B'rith, and the religious movements, as well as over one hundred local JCRCs, Jewish Community Relations Committees or Councils. As the lead professional on Israel at the JCPA, my task was to identify and nurture consensus positions that would guide the advocacy efforts of this diverse network. It wasn't easy, and it became exponentially more challenging following the signing of the Oslo Accords in 1993.

There was strong resistance to the Accords, not just from right-leaning Israelis but from among wide segments of the American Jewish community as well. Nevertheless, we did achieve consensus in support of the peace process. In 1994, JCPA became the first Jewish organization to visit Yasser Arafat in Gaza after he relocated there from Tunis. Our board even hosted him at a meeting in New York City in 1995, for which we received a good deal of criticism from some quarters. We believed that if Israel's elected leadership was prepared to normalize relations with him and the PLO, the American Jewish community should be prepared to do so as well.

The future of Jerusalem, one of the final status issues to be negotiated by the parties, was a hot potato. Feelings that Israel should never relinquish control over the city ran strong. In 1994, JCPA adopted a resolution that expressed "the unified commitment of world Jewry to maintain the city of Jerusalem as the eternal undivided capital of Israel ... and to increase its efforts to educate American policymakers and the public about the unique status of Jerusalem in the life of Israel and world Jewry."

Then, in March 2000, JCPA applauded then Prime Minister Ehud Barak's "call for intensive negotiations with the Palestinians to lead to a final status agreement... In these final status negotiations, Israel and the Palestinians will face the most challenging issues of the Oslo process, including the future of Jerusalem…."

When asked by colleagues how I reconciled these two positions, I observed, "The 1994 resolution expressed a conviction. At the same time, just as the Palestinians have a conviction about the right of refugees to return to their homes inside Israel, the parties will have to negotiate an agreement both can accept. That's the underlying meaning of the 2000 resolution."

The Oslo process, which started out with great hope, eventually ended in failure. What and who were to blame? Yitzhak Rabin's assassination? The terrorist bombings on Jerusalem's Number 18 buses that killed dozens of Israelis—a bus line I frequently used in the 1970s—which in 1996 helped bring to power Benjamin Netanyahu, an opponent of Oslo? The bloody second intifada, which erupted following the failure of negotiations at Camp David? All the above? Books have been written on this topic. At the end of the Camp David Summit, Arafat stunned President Bill Clinton when he declared, "There is nothing there," regarding the ancient Jewish temple, thus seeking to delegitimize the Jewish people's connection to Jerusalem. Whatever belief Israelis initially had in Arafat's positive intentions melted away. Decimated, Israel's peace camp has yet to recover from these multiple body blows.

Almost all Jewish and Arab Israeli children study in their own schools. This is not because of a forced segregation policy, but rather a matter of choice. But there are parents who want their children to be together, and a modest number of Hand-in-Hand schools have been established around Israel that offer a dual curriculum and equal language study for Hebrew and Arabic. On one of my JCPA missions to Israel in 2008, shortly after Obama was elected president, our delegation met with children in one such school in Jerusalem. There was much interest in Obama as America's first black president.

One little Arab girl innocently asked whether I thought an Arab might become prime minister of Israel one day. My answer: "Why not? Obama's victory shows that everything is possible." I thought to myself … maybe, but it would have to be a fundamentally different Israel. But what also made a deep impression on me was the fact that our brief conversation was conducted in Hebrew. I made a vow that day to study Arabic so if a similar situation arose, I could respond in her native language. In fact, many years later, I studied Arabic for two semesters at Rutgers University. Fluent in Hebrew, I had a leg up on the young college students sitting next to me in class as the two languages share many similarities.

After retiring from JCPA in 2014, I continued to consult for various Jewish organizations, including the Israel Policy Forum (IPF). IPF, in my judgment, strikes the right balance of support for the two-state outcome, concern for Israel's security, and readiness at times to criticize both Israeli and Palestinian governments. I also helped the Alliance for Middle East Peace (ALLMEP) in its quest for funding in support of Israeli-Palestinian people-to-people programs.

Today, freed of the requirement to be non-partisan, I have become deeply involved with efforts in my native Pennsylvania to elect Democrats up and down the ballot. My motivation stems from a conviction that a Donald Trump-dominated Republican Party poses a clear and present threat to American democracy. I also believe that, of the two parties, Democrats are much more committed to encouraging Israel and the Palestinians to resolve their conflict.

Reflections
Sometimes, I wonder what trajectory my life would have taken had I chosen to attend co-ed Muhlenberg College (#2 choice) instead of F&M. Perhaps, satisfied with its social environment, I might not have pursued a junior year abroad. I might have

gone straight to an American law school and then developed a professional career here, completely unrelated to Israel.

What I do know, for sure, is that Jerusalem immediately captured me in the fall of 1968, and over half a century later it has never let me go. This doesn't happen to every Jew who spends periods of time there. Clearly, there was some added ingredient in me—my identity, my family, my personality—that combined with this special place to create a lifelong impact. Clearly, family did play a major role. How else to explain that my younger brother and only sibling, David, harbored his own lifelong Zionist dream? Now, in his late 60s, he immigrated to Israel several years ago and is happily living in Netanya.

After having children, I eagerly awaited the time when we could take a family trip to Israel. We did this in May 2000 when our daughter Alanna turned 13 years old, and our son Josh turned 10. We traveled the land from north to south and everywhere in between for three weeks. I knew the highlight of the trip would be Jerusalem. I meticulously prepared a visit that would at least give them a small taste of the magic I had experienced decades before. Subsequently, both children and Josh's wife Nicole (girlfriend at the time) visited Israel on Birthright trips during their college years. Nicole subsequently worked for Hillel, the Jewish students' organization, and led many Birthright trips. Alanna spent almost six months on a Tel Aviv-based career enhancement program.

Our first grandchild, Hallie Maya, entered the world and our lives in May 2022. As an expression of our Jewish concept of *L'dor v'dor*, "from generation to generation," will I be blessed to live a long and healthy enough life to be able to take her to Israel and Jerusalem, maybe as her Bat Mitzvah gift? Only time will tell.

And should Hallie Maya and I visit in the year 2034-5, will there be two states between the Jordan River and Mediterranean Sea, a Jewish and democratic State of Israel, and a democratic

State of Palestine, existing side by side in peace and security? And will those two states have found a creative and mutually acceptable way of sharing an undivided City of Jerusalem? As my Arabic-speaking friends say, *Inshallah.*

CONTRIBUTORS

EDITORS

Dr. Carole Monica C. Burnett serves on the Board of Directors of the Jerusalem Peace Institute. She is the Advocacy Outreach Coordinator at the Holy Land Christian Ecumenical Foundation (HCEF) and the co-Chair of the HCEF Research and Publication Committee. She is the editor of the Fathers of the Church series, an expanding collection of early Christian texts translated from Greek, Latin, and Syriac, published by the Catholic University of America Press. Burnett is co-editor of *What Jerusalem Means to Us: Muslim Perspectives and Reflections*. She has retired from teaching Church History at the Ecumenical Institute of Theology of St. Mary's Seminary & University in Baltimore, as well as Greek and Latin at the Dominican House of Studies in Washington, D.C.

Dr. Saliba Sarsar is co-Founder and President of the Jerusalem Peace Institute. He is Professor of Political Science at Monmouth University and Visiting Research Collaborator at Princeton University. His teaching and scholarly interests focus on the Middle East, Palestinian-Israeli affairs, Jerusalem, and peacebuilding. His most recent authored books are *Peacebuilding in Israeli-Palestinian Relations* and *Jerusalem: The Home in Our Hearts*. His most recent edited books are *The Holy Land Confederation as a Facilitator for the Two-State Solution* and *What Jerusalem Means to Us: Christian Perspectives and Reflections*. His most recent co-edited books are *Inequality and Governance in an Uncertain World: Perspectives on Democratic & Autocratic Governments*; *Democracy in Crisis Around the World*; *Continuity and Change in Political Culture: Israel and Beyond*, and *What Jerusalem Means to Us: Muslim Perspectives and Reflections*. Dr. Sarsar is the recipient of the Award of Academic Excellence from the American Task Force on Palestine, the Global Visionary Award and the Stafford Presidential Award of Excellence from Monmouth University, the Humanitarian Award from the National Conference for Community and Justice, and the Holy Land Christian Ecumenical Foundation Award.

AUTHOR OF THE PREFACE

Rateb Y. Rabie, KCHS is the Founder and President/CEO of the Holy Land Christian Ecumenical Foundation (HCEF), Founder and President of the Know Thy Heritage (KTH) Leadership Initiative, and co-Founder of the Jerusalem Peace Institute (JPI) and Chair of its Board of Directors. Born in Amman, Jordan, to Palestinian parents, he is co-founder and past national president of the Birzeit Society and co-founder, Vice President, and Treasurer of the Institute for Health, Development, and Research in Palestine. He is also a Knight Commander of the Equestrian Order of the Holy Sepulchre and a 4th Degree Knight of Columbus, founder and co-chair of the Holy Land Outreach Committee of the Knights of Columbus (K of C), Maryland State Council. He is recipient of the Faith and Tolerance Award from the Arab American Anti-Discrimination Committee (ADC). Sir Rateb is committed to improving the living conditions for Palestinian Christians in their homeland, preserving Palestine's Christian heritage, and strengthening the identity of Palestinian Christians in the worldwide diaspora.

AUTHORS OF THE ESSAYS

Dr. Yael S. Aronoff holds the Michael and Elaine Serling and Friends Endowed Chair in Israel Studies and serves as the director of the Michael and Elaine Serling Institute for Jewish Studies and Modern Israel at Michigan State University, and as a professor of Political Science at James Madison College at Michigan State University. Her primary research and work focus on Israeli politics and foreign policy, Israeli society and culture, the Israeli-Palestinian conflict and efforts to resolve it, and Israel's asymmetric wars. She is particularly interested in peace negotiations and the conditions under which wars end, as well as the means and limits of war. Among Aronoff's publications are the book, *The Political Psychology of Israeli Prime Ministers: When Hard Liners Opt for Peace*, and the co-edited book, *Continuity and Change in Political Culture: Israel and Beyond*. Her current book project is titled, *The Dilemmas of Asymmetric Conflicts: Navigating Deterrence and Democratic Constraints*. Dr. Aronoff has published in *Foreign Policy, Israel Studies, Israel Studies Review,* and *Political Science Quarterly*; she is past President of the Association of Israel Studies and has given over 100 public lectures.

Dr. Aleen Z. Bayard is on the faculty of Northwestern University, where she teaches courses on leadership and organizational change. Through her studies in peacebuilding, she earned her doctorate in Values Driven Leadership from Benedictine University. Dr. Bayard is the founder of a consulting practice supporting organizations committed to enriching and empowering the workplace as a source of individual and societal transformation. Outside of her academic and professional activities, she invests her energy in causes to achieve social justice and peace on a global scale. She is happily married and is a proud mother of two sons.

Dr. Elan Ezrachi is a Jerusalem-based consultant and independent scholar of the relations between Jewish Diasporas and Israel. His book, *Awakened Dream: 50 Years of Complex Unification of Jerusalem*, was published in 2017. Dr. Elan served in various executive roles, including Director of the International Department of Melitz –Center for Jewish Zionist Education, Director of the Charles Bronfman Mifgashim Center, Executive Director of Masa Israel Journey, and Director of the International School for Jerusalem Studies at Yad Ben-Zvi. He is an active player in the Israeli Jewish Renaissance scene and was the founding chair of Panim for Jewish Renaissance in Israel.

Dr. Jonathan Golden, Assistant Professor of Religious Studies in the departments of Comparative Religion and Anthropology at Drew University, holds several certificates in conflict resolution and works closely with interfaith and peace organizations in New Jersey and around the world. As author of *Ancient Canaan and Israel: New Perspectives* and the forthcoming *Dawn of the Metal Age*, he is currently working on a third book based on interviews with ex-combatants and victims of conflict who have become peace activists. In addition to leading the Conflict Resolution program, Dr. Golden is director of Drew's Center on Religion, Culture, and Conflict, an interdisciplinary center focused on global peacebuilding and interfaith leadership.

Rabbi Naamah Kelman is a descendant of 10 generations of rabbis, becoming in 1992 the first woman to be ordained by the Hebrew Union College (HUC) in Jerusalem, where she is currently the Dean. Born and raised in New York, she has lived in Israel since 1976, where she has worked in community organizing, Jewish education, and the promotion and establishment of Progressive and Pluralistic Judaism for Israelis. Rabbi Kelman has been intensely involved in the emerging education system of the Israeli Movement for Progressive (Reform) Judaism. Among the founders of the first Progressive day school, she has overseen the development of curricular materials, teacher training programs, and family education. She has been involved in the professional development of Israeli Rabbinic students, and the establishment of the Blaustein Center for Spiritual Counseling. She has served as the Director of the Year in Israel Program for HUC's North American students. Kelman is deeply engaged in inter-faith dialogue and feminist causes.

Professor Menachem Klein is Professor Emeritus in the Department of Political Science at Bar-Ilan University, Israel. He pursued Middle East and Islamic Studies at the Hebrew University of Jerusalem. Since 1996, he has been active in many unofficial negotiations with Palestinian counterparts. In October 2003, Prof. Klein signed, together with prominent Israeli and Palestinian negotiators, the Geneva Agreement—a detailed proposal for a comprehensive Israeli-Palestinian peace accord. Among Prof. Klein's books are *Arafat and Abbas: Portraits of Leadership in a State Postponed; Lives in Common—Arabs and Jews in Jerusalem, Jaffa and Hebron*; *The Shift: Israel-Palestine from Border Conflict to Ethnic Struggle*; *Jerusalem: The Contested City*; *The Jerusalem Problem: The Struggle for Permanent Status*; and *A Possible Peace Between Israel and Palestine: An Insider's Account of the Geneva Initiative*. In addition, he is the author of eight books in Hebrew and 63 journal articles and chapters in books both in Hebrew and in English.

Rabbi Ron Kronish served for 24 years as the founder and director of a major interreligious institution in Jerusalem, the Interreligious Coordinating Council in Israel. His latest book, *Profiles in Peace: Voices of Peacebuilders in the Midst of the Israeli-Palestinian Conflict*, was published this year. Previously, he wrote *The Other Peace Process* (Hamilton Books, 2017), and he edited *Coexistence and Reconciliation in Israel* (Paulist Press, 2015). He blogs for *The Times of Israel* (https://blogs.timesofisrael.com/author/ron-kronish/) and is a regular contributor to *The Jerusalem Report*. In addition, he is an adjunct lecturer at Drew University's Theological School and at the Schechter Institute for Jewish Studies in Jerusalem. For more about him and his work, see www.ronkronish.com.

Dr. Yehezkel Landau, a dual Israeli-American citizen, is an interfaith educator, leadership trainer, author, and consultant working to promote Jewish-Christian-Muslim engagement and Israeli-Palestinian peacebuilding for more than 40 years. While living in Jerusalem, he directed the *OZ veSHALOM-NETIVOT SHALOM* religious peace movement during the 1980s, and from 1991 to 2003, he co-founded and co-directed the OPEN HOUSE Center for Jewish-Arab Coexistence and Reconciliation in Ramle, *www.friendsofopenhouse.co.il*. From 2002 to 2016, Dr. Landau was a professor of Jewish tradition and interfaith relations at Hartford Seminary, where he held the Chair in Abrahamic Partnerships and directed the Building Abrahamic Partnerships training program for Jews, Christians, and Muslims. His publications include the co-edited book, *Voices From Jerusalem: Jews and Christians Reflect on the Holy Land*, and a U. S. Institute of Peace research report, titled *Healing The Holy Land: Interreligious Peacebuilding In Israel/Palestine*. Dr. Landau earned an A.B. from Harvard University, an M.T.S. from Harvard Divinity School, and a D. Min. from Hartford Seminary. Additional information can be found at *www.landau-interfaith.com*.

Rabbi Laurence P. Malinger graduated from Southern Methodist University with a Bachelor of Science degree in Applied Mathematics in 1987. He completed graduate work at Trinity University, earning the Master of Education with School Psychology in 1988. He received his Master of Arts in Hebrew Letters degree and was ordained Rabbi in 1992 and 1993, respectively, from the Hebrew Union College, Jewish Institute of Religion, Cincinnati, Ohio. Upon ordination, Rabbi Malinger became Assistant Rabbi and Director of Education at Congregation Beth Emeth in Wilmington, Delaware. He was promoted to Associate Rabbi in July 1997. In June 1999, Rabbi Malinger was elected as senior Rabbi of Temple Shalom of Aberdeen, New Jersey. He is a member of the Central Conference of American Rabbis (CCAR) and proudly serves as an advisor for the Monmouth Center for World Religions and Ethical Thought (MCWRET).

Dr. Ilan Peleg is a former President of the Association for Israel Studies (AIS) and the Founding Editor-in-Chief of *Israel Studies Forum* (now *Israel Studies Review*), the scholarly journal of the AIS. He is the author of over 100 scholarly articles, and the editor or author of 15 books, including *Democratizing the Hegemonic State* (Cambridge University Press, 2007) and *Israel's Palestinians: The Conflict Within* (also CUP, 2011, with Dov Waxman). Additional books include a volume on the foreign policy of Menachem Begin, a book on bi-national Israel, an edited book on multidisciplinary perspectives on the Middle East peace process, a book on George W. Bush's foreign policy and Neo-Conservatism, and more. Dr. Peleg has delivered hundreds of lectures in many forums and has appeared on CNN, Voice of America, National Public Radio, and other media platforms.

Mr. Martin J. Raffel, Esq., served for 27 years as senior vice president and lead professional on Israel and other international issues for the New York-based Jewish Council for Public Affairs (JCPA) until his retirement in 2014. Prior to that, he worked as director of the American Jewish Congress and assistant director of the American Jewish Committee in Philadelphia. Mr. Raffel, who is widely published in the Jewish and general press, spent seven years in Jerusalem, where he studied at Hebrew University's School of Law and worked in Israel's Ministry of Justice. He is married and lives in Bucks County, Pennsylvania.

Rabbi Peretz Rodman is an American-born Israeli educator, writer, and translator. A graduate of Brandeis University and Boston's Hebrew College, he was ordained by the Schechter Rabbinical Seminary in Jerusalem. Rabbi Rodman has taught Hebrew and Jewish studies at every level from elementary school to graduate school, as well as at Hebrew and Christian theological schools. He has published over 100 popular and academic articles in Jewish studies. Today, he serves as head of the rabbinical court (*av be din*) of the Masorti (Conservative) rabbinate in Israel.

Ms. Sharon Rosen is Director of Religious Engagement at Search for Common Ground (Search), the world's largest organization dedicated to peacebuilding, working on the frontlines of today's most consequential conflicts. An expert on interreligious programming and advancing religious freedom, Ms. Rosen provides strategic oversight, quality control, and technical expertise to Search's field offices in more than 20 countries including Jerusalem, where she directs a Jewish-Muslim religious leaders' initiative to expand *Constituencies for Peace* within religious communities in Israel. Previously for ten years she co-directed, with a Palestinian colleague,

Search's Jerusalem office, leading multiple cross-border projects in religion, development, health, and media.

Rabbi John L. Rosove is Senior Rabbi Emeritus of Temple Israel of Hollywood in Los Angeles, a national co-chair of the Rabbinic and Cantorial Cabinet of J Street, and past national chair of the Association of Reform Zionists of America (ARZA). He is the author of two books: *Why Judaism Matters—Letters of a Liberal Rabbi to his Children and the Millennial Generation* (Nashville: Jewish Lights, 2017) and *Why Israel [and its Future] Matters—Letters of a Liberal Rabbi to his Children and the Millennial Generation* (New Jersey: Ben Yehuda Press, 2019), each with Afterwords by his sons Daniel and David.

Dr. Alice Rothchild, a physician, author, and filmmaker, is focused on human rights and social justice in Israel/Palestine. As an obstetrician-gynecologist, she practiced clinical medicine and served as Assistant Professor of Obstetrics and Gynecology at the Harvard Medical School. She writes and lectures widely and is the author of books, including *Broken Promises, Broken Dreams: Stories of Jewish and Palestinian Trauma and Resilience* and *Condition Critical: Life and Death in Israel/Palestine*, and the young adult novel, *Finding Melody Sullivan*. She has contributed to several anthologies, the most recent being *Reclaiming Judaism from Zionism: Stories of Personal Transformation.* She directed a documentary film, *Voices Across the Divide,* and is active in Jewish Voice for Peace and We Are Not Numbers.

Dr. Tamar Verete-Zahavi was born in 1959 in Jerusalem, where she now lives with her family. She studied education, psychology, and psychoanalysis at the University of Paris VII, where she received a Ph.D. for her study of socio-political images in children. Dr. Verete-Zahavi has worked for many years in Education-for-Tolerance between Jews and Arabs. Together with Abedalsalam Yunis, she has published two bilingual children's books, and has won—together with him—the Jerusalem Foundation Award for Furthering Tolerance in the city. Verete-Zahavi was also awarded an Andersen Honor Citation in 2016.

APPENDIX I

JPI JERUSALEM PEACE INSTITUTE

Jerusalem is unique among the cities of the world. Its distinctiveness stems from its holiness and universal character. An important place of spiritual attachment for Muslims, Christians, and Jews, its religious and political aspects are intertwined. Its status requires of all to think and act creatively, sensitively, and responsibly about its future so that it can be a source of peace and harmony between peoples and religions.

Our interest in Jerusalem dates back for decades. It is an essential part of who we are, with some of us being born and raised in Jerusalem, with all of us connected in ways historical, spiritual, religious, and cultural to this beautiful Holy City and deep feeling of belonging. Still others have come to love the city from near or afar, as it is connected to their Jerusalem family and relatives, sense of humanity, faith traditions, national aspirations, entrepreneurial pursuits, and/ or intellectual quests.

Core Values: peace, justice, equality, inclusion, economic resilience, cultural heritage, accountable leadership

Vision: Jerusalem is a gift for humanity. Its sharing and inclusivity are a must for charting a new beginning.

Principles of Our Vision:

1. Jerusalem is truly central to the three faith traditions of Judaism, Christianity, and Islam and to others; its soul and spirit embrace all of them, equally.

2. Jerusalem is essential for justice, peace, equality, and reconciliation between Israelis and Palestinians and in our world.

3. All of Jerusalem's inhabitants deserve to live a dignified life, in peace and equality, with the ability to freely pursue and develop their daily lives, including access to adequate housing, jobs, education, medical care, municipal services, religious sites, and cultural activities.

4. All of Jerusalem's inhabitants are entitled to their fundamental human rights and legal protection according to international law, including as enshrined in the Universal Declaration of Human Rights and United Nations resolutions.

Mission: The Jerusalem Peace Institute highlights Jerusalem as humanity's shared gift governed by two peoples and cherished by three faiths, and its centrality for a just peace through advocacy, programs, activities, interdisciplinary research, and publications.

www.jerusalem-pi.org

www.ingramcontent.com/pod-product-compliance
Lightning Source LLC
Chambersburg PA
CBHW060947050426
42337CB00052B/1635